W9-BNK-651

Reading
for
Proficiency

A Test Preparation Program

Level A

GLOBE FEARON EDUCATIONAL PUBLISHER
Upper Saddle River, New Jersey
www.globefearon.com

Reviewers:

Bettye J. Birden
Language Arts Department Chairperson
Houston Independent School District
Houston, Texas

Sally Parker, M.A.
Language Arts Resource Teacher
Elk Grove Unified School District
Sacramento, California

Executive Editor: Jean Liccione
Project Editor: Kim Choi
Senior Editor: Lynn Kloss
Production Editor: Alan Dalgleish
Designer: Jennifer Visco
Composition: Phyllis Rosinsky

Copyright © 1999 by Globe Fearon, Inc. One Lake Street, Upper Saddle River, New Jersey 07458. All rights reserved. No part of this book may be reproduced or transmitted in any form or by any means, electronic, photographic, mechanical, or otherwise, including photocopying, recording, or by any information storage and retrieval system, without permission in writing from the publisher.

Printed in the United States of America
3 4 5 6 7 8 9 10 02 01 00 99

ISBN: 0-835-94858-7

GLOBE FEARON EDUCATIONAL PUBLISHER
Upper Saddle River, New Jersey
www.globefearon.com

CONTENTS

CONTENTS

INTRODUCTION
Succeeding on the Reading Test

Soon you'll be taking a reading test. So will many other students. There are three big questions that most students wonder about as they prepare for a test:

1. What's going to be on the test?
2. How can this book help me succeed on the test?
3. How can I get a good score on the test?

The main purpose of this book is to answer these questions.

 BIG QUESTION 1: WHAT'S GOING TO BE ON THE TEST?
The test will have four different types of reading passages. You'll need special skills and strategies to read each passage and answer the questions.

A. Different Kinds of Reading Passages on the Test
Here are the four types of reading passages you'll find on the test:

- **Narrative text** is writing that tells a story. Stories and novels are the most common narrative texts.

- **Informational text** is writing that mainly gives information about a topic. Your science and social studies textbooks are examples of informational text.

- **Persuasive text** is writing that tries to persuade you to do or to think something. Editorials, letters to the editor, and advertisements are examples of persuasive text.

- **Everyday text** is the type of writing you see every day. Food labels, sets of directions, and lists of rules are examples of this kind of text.

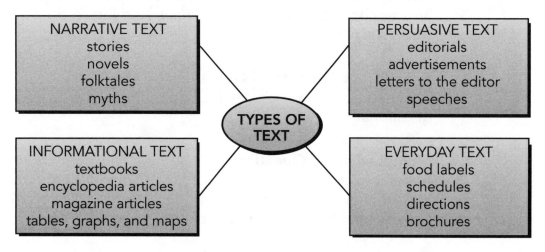

B. Different Levels of Questions on the Test

Each reading passage on the test is followed by multiple-choice questions. You can answer some of these questions by simply reading the lines of the text. To answer other questions, you'll need to "read between the lines" or even "read beyond the lines," using your own background and what you already know.

Reading the Lines

The answers to many questions are stated directly in the reading passage. All you need to do is read the lines carefully. For example, a narrative passage might be about 12-year-old Don and his 10-year-old sister Anna. Together, they walk 8 miles on the June 14 Walkathon to raise money for the homeless. A multiple-choice question might ask whether Anna is 8, 10, 12, or 14 years old. By reading the lines carefully, you can find the correct answer.

Reading Between the Lines

The answers to some questions are not stated directly in the text. These answers are only *implied* in the text. To figure out the answer yourself, you'll have to use details in the text as well as what you know from real life. For example, a story might describe a group of children hiding in a room with balloons, presents, and a cake. They're all waiting quietly for one person to arrive. Although the author doesn't say it directly, you can figure out that a surprise party is about to begin. The story details and what you already know let you read between the lines.

Reading Beyond the Lines

A few questions may ask you to take a word or idea from a test passage and use it in another situation. For example, an article might suggest that a community or region is in "dire straits" due to an inadequate supply of water. A question about this passage might ask you to decide which of the four different situations listed in the answer choices is also an example of someone or something in "dire straits." These answer choices, however, would have nothing to do with inadequate water supplies.

C. Different Formats of Questions on the Test

The reading test will usually include multiple-choice and open-ended questions.

Multiple-Choice Questions

A multiple-choice question gives you a statement and four possible answer choices. Only one of the four choices is correct. The test will have several types of multiple-choice questions.

- **Complete-Sentence Questions** This type of question is a complete sentence. Each answer choice is a complete sentence, too.

> Why are today's bikes faster than ones built before 1900?
> - A. They have pedals connected to the front wheels.
> - B. The front and rear tires are the same size.
> - C. They have gears.
> - D. They have inflated tires.

- **Sentence-Completion Questions** This type of question is not a complete sentence. Instead, you have to choose the answer that best completes the opening statement.

> At the beginning of the story, Jimmy seems to be
> - A. ruthless and ambitious.
> - B. very intelligent.
> - C. dishonest and lazy.
> - D. steady and predictable.

- **Special-Wording Questions** Some questions are worded in ways that require special attention. For example, they may ask you to choose the *best* or *most likely* answer. That means that you'll have to judge which one of several possible answers is the best one.

> Based on what you've read, Jean would MOST LIKELY be a successful
> - A. writer.
> - B. businessperson.
> - C. doctor.
> - D. lawyer.

- **Vocabulary Questions** Vocabulary questions ask about the meanings of words in the passage. Usually, you will have to read between the lines and use clues in the passage to figure out the word's meaning.

> In paragraph 3 of this passage, the word **terrain** means
> - A. the moon's surface.
> - B. a kind of turtle.
> - C. a piece of land.
> - D. a flat roof.

Some vocabulary questions ask about multiple-meaning words. The answer choices will show a word's four different meanings.

Open-Ended Questions

Open-ended questions ask you to write answers in your own words on special writing lines. The questions can be answered in many different ways. Open-ended questions are an opportunity to show what you know and express your own ideas.

You will usually begin an open-ended answer with a statement of your main idea. The rest of the answer will be details and examples that support your main idea.

> How would you describe the theme, or main message, of "Cinderella"?
>
> "Cinderella" illustrates the theme that the good are rewarded in the end. Cinderella, who has been treated cruelly by her stepmother and stepsisters, is helped by her fairy godmother to attend the ball at the palace. At the ball, the prince recognizes her beauty and goodness, and Cinderella becomes queen.

BIG QUESTION 2: HOW CAN THIS BOOK HELP ME SUCCEED ON THE TEST?

This book is organized and designed with you in mind. All of the features described below will help you do well on your next reading test.

- **Chapter Openers** Each chapter introduction gives you an overview of one of the types of reading found on tests. The introductions also answer the questions you're most likely to ask about these types of texts. Finally, you'll see some typical questions taken from actual tests.

- **Lessons** The lessons in each chapter focus on the skills you will need on reading tests. Each lesson also includes some valuable test-taking tips. After answering the questions in the first part of a lesson, you can check your own answers. The book explains those answers and why they are right or wrong. You can then use the skills you learned in completing the second part of the lesson.

- **Chapter Tests** At the end of each chapter, you'll find a reading test. This test focuses on the type of text presented in the chapter. Here's a chance to work with all the skills in the chapter at once. The clock symbol on the test shows you how much time you have to answer the questions.

- **Practice Test** After you've worked through the four chapters, you can try the Practice Test. It has four parts—one for each type of text. The Practice Test is very similar to the reading test you'll take.

- **Reading Comprehension Skills Mini-Lessons** Check out the nine mini-lessons at the back of the book. They review many of the important reading skills that will help you answer test questions.

- **Glossary** The last page of the book is a glossary. That's where to check the meaning of the special words and terms in this book.

 BIG QUESTION 3: HOW CAN I GET A GOOD SCORE ON THE TEST?
By completing this book, you'll take a giant step toward scoring high on your next reading test. It is important to answer the following questions before and during the test. The more *Yes* answers you have, the more successful you'll be!

Answering Questions
✔ Did I read the question carefully?
✔ Did I study all of the possible answers?
✔ Did I eliminate the obvious wrong answers before guessing at the correct one?

Managing Time
✔ Is there a clock to help me use my time well?
✔ Do I know how much time to give to each part of the test?
✔ Am I working quickly and steadily?

Completing the Answer Sheet
✔ Am I sure I understand how to fill in answers?
✔ Have I looked over the answer sheet?
✔ Did I fill in the oval that corresponds to my answer choice?
✔ Did I fill in the oval darkly and completely?
✔ Did I fill in only one oval for each answer?
✔ Before changing an answer, did I completely erase the old answer?

Doing My Personal Best
✔ Did I get a good night's rest before the test?
✔ Did I wake up early and eat a good breakfast?
✔ Did I collect my thoughts and relax before the test?
✔ Do I have confidence in myself?

Narrative text will be part of almost every formal reading test you take. Here are some common questions about this important type of writing.

 What is a narrative text?
Any writing that tells a story is a narrative text.

 What types of reading materials are narrative texts?
The most common types of narrative text are short stories and novels. It may also take the form of myths, folktales, essays, and even poems. Regardless of the form, a narrative text tells a story in a connected series of events.

 What are the major elements of narrative text?
The major elements of narrative text are character, plot, setting, and theme.

- **Characters** are the people in a story or novel. Each character has certain qualities, or character traits, that the reader discovers as the story unfolds.

- The **plot** is the sequence of events that happens in a story or novel. Usually the plot includes a problem that a character solves.

- The **setting** is the time and place in which the action of a story takes place. Being aware of the setting will help you understand a story.

- The **theme** of a story is the main idea or message that the author wants you to think about or learn. A theme of a story might be that "it pays to be generous" or "there are many ways to solve a problem."

All the elements of a narrative text work together to tell a story.

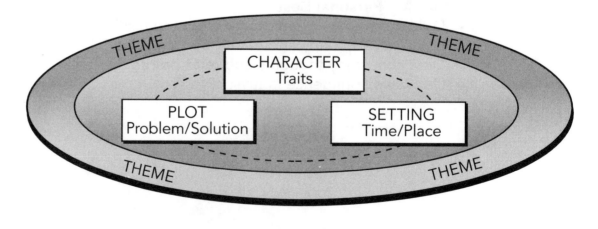

Test Questions About Narrative Text

Most test questions about narrative text focus on character, plot, setting, and theme. Although these questions take many different forms, certain types of questions are common. The questions below come from actual tests. Study them carefully. They will help you become familiar with the most common types of test questions that are asked about narrative text.

Questions About Characters

- Who is telling the story?
- Which words BEST describe Carlo?
- How does Juan feel at the end of the story?
- What is Anita's main character trait?
- How would you describe Mr. Chen's role in the story?
- What conclusion can you draw about Mrs. Reilly?

Questions About Plot

- Which event happens first in the story?
- What is the main problem, or conflict, in the story?
- Why was Jerry embarrassed at school?
- Which event occurred before Chita arrived?
- What is the high point, or climax, of the story?
- How is the main problem resolved in the story?

Questions About Setting

- When does the action in this story take place?
- Where does the action in this story take place?
- About how much time passes before Angela meets Rene?
- How would you describe the village in the story?
- Which feature of the location affects the pioneers most?
- Why is it important that this story is set in 1945?

Questions About Theme

- What is the main idea of this story?
- Which statement BEST expresses the message of the story?
- With which of the following opinions would the author PROBABLY agree?
- What lesson does the author want readers to learn?
- Why do you think the author ended the story in this way?

The lessons in Chapter 1 will help you understand how to answer test questions about character, plot, setting, and theme. You'll read some short passages from stories and answer a few questions. The questions will help you focus on these important elements of narrative text.

Lesson 1 Character

Characters are the people in a story or novel. As a story unfolds, each character reveals certain qualities, or **character traits**. A character's words, thoughts, and actions usually show these traits. Sometimes an author states the character's traits directly. Another character in a story can also tell you what a character is like.

When you read about a story character, use all the details supplied by the author to form a general idea of the character. Then, when you answer questions about the character, compare each answer choice with your own ideas.

Tips for Success
- Always use details from the story to support the answers you choose.
- The actions, words, and thoughts of a character help you understand him or her.

This passage is about a teenager who wants to be an artist. Use the details you read to form a general idea of what she is like.

The July she turned 13, Sonia began setting artistic goals for herself. In large letters, she printed her first "objective" in her journal: Use pink and yellow to portray a sun that really shines. Then, day after day, Sonia trekked out into the desert to paint the sunlight on the mesas. Despite the 100-degree heat, her solemn brown eyes shone, and the tiny smile rarely left her lips. It took a dozen tries, but at last . . . . "That's it!" she cried. "Yes, that's the sunlight shining on the stone!" After hanging the painting in her room, Sonia opened her journal and printed: "Objective 2: Use black and lavender to show moonlight on the sand."

1. Which statement BEST describes Sonia?
   A. Sonia loved nature very much and spent much time outdoors.
   B. Sonia seemed more interested in living a glamorous, artistic life than in expressing herself with paint and canvas.
   C. Sonia's determined effort to paint brought her satisfaction.
   D. Sonia was a very talented artist whose paintings of the desert inspired her family and friends.

1. Ⓐ Ⓑ Ⓒ Ⓓ **Mark your answer choice by filling in the oval.**

✓ **Now check to see whether you chose the correct answer.**

A. This statement may be true, because Sonia did spend time outdoors; however, it is not the best description.

B. This statement is untrue. Sonia worked very hard to express herself as an artist.

C. This is the correct answer. All the details in the paragraph support this description.

D. This information is not mentioned in the paragraph and cannot be used to answer the question.

This passage is about two sixth-grade boys on a class field trip. As you read, use all the details to form a general idea of each character.

During a trip to the art museum, the sixth graders were eating bag lunches in the sculpture garden. Feeling bored, Ted whispered, "Hey Benny, let's sneak out for pizza."

"But it's against the rules to—" Benny began.

"Rules are made to be broken," Ted **smirked** with a self-satisfied expression on his face, and he darted toward the busy road. Car brakes squealed as the short 12-year-old jaywalked over to the pizza parlor. Inside, he brushed past an elderly couple who were waiting to order. "One slice!" he shouted, pointing at the clerk. "I'm in a hurry!"

Meanwhile, Benny waited for the green light and crossed the street. "I really should stay with the class," he thought, but Benny was new in town, and so far Ted was his only friend.

Benny entered the restaurant. "A slice of pizza, please," he ordered.

"Benny!" Ted bellowed across the room. His mouth was full of pizza, and sauce was dripping onto his shirt. "Buy me another slice, and I'll pay you back the money I owe you."

Mark the best answer for questions 1–4.

1. Ⓐ Ⓑ Ⓒ Ⓓ
2. Ⓐ Ⓑ Ⓒ Ⓓ
3. Ⓐ Ⓑ Ⓒ Ⓓ
4. Ⓐ Ⓑ Ⓒ Ⓓ

1. Ted's actions show that he
   A. has a good sense of humor.
   B. is a true friend to Benny.
   C. tends to be a show-off.
   D. tries to behave properly.

2. The word **smirked** in the third paragraph means
   A. walked away.
   B. whispered.
   C. laughed loudly.
   D. smiled in a smug way.

3. Benny tends to be
   A. independent-minded.
   B. quite proud.
   C. unsure of himself.
   D. fun-loving.

4. Benny PROBABLY goes with Ted for pizza because
   A. he forgot to bring a lunch.
   B. he wants to stay friends with Ted.
   C. Ted owes him money.
   D. he doesn't like the museum.

5. Do you think Benny will stay friends with Ted? Explain your answer.

_____

_____

_____

_____

Lesson 2 Plot

A **plot** is a series of events that make up a story. The plot is "what happens" in the story. Most plots center on a **problem** that a character faces. Usually the plot shows the **solution** or how the problem is solved.

In the fairy tale "Beauty and the Beast," for example, Beauty has a problem. She feels trapped in a castle with someone who looks like a beast. She solves the problem by making friends with the Beast and learning to understand him.

Tips for Success

- Pay attention to how each story event leads to the next.
- Look for the main problem the character must solve.
- Focus on how the problem is solved.

As you read this passage, think about how the story events are related. Also, look for the problem that Tomás has.

When Tomás moved to Linwood Acres, all the houses in the development looked alike. That didn't bother Tomás. That is, it didn't bother him until the night Miguel's dad dropped him off at 1:30 A.M. after a camping trip.

Tomás let himself in the front door, surprised that his parents had left it unlocked. He didn't turn on the lights. No sense waking everyone up. "Whew! The house stinks like cigars," he thought. "I hope Tio Alfredo isn't here!" Bounding upstairs, Tomás turned on the light in his bedroom. What? Where were his posters, his desk, and his bunkbeds? And why was Louie García from next door sleeping here?

"Oh, no!" said Tomás, realizing his mistake. Hurrying outside, he raced to the next door. This time he looked for the name "Rodriguez" on the door before going in.

1. What is Tomás's main problem in the story?

   A. Miguel's dad has dropped him off far too late at night.

   B. He doesn't like Linwood Acres because all the houses look alike.

   C. Someone has taken the posters, desk, and bed from his room.

   D. He has gone into Louie García's house by mistake.

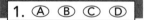

Mark your answer choice by filling in the oval.

Now check to see whether you chose the correct answer.

   A. Getting home late isn't the problem, although it may have added to the problem.

   B. The story says the look-alike houses don't bother Tomás.

   C. This isn't the problem. For a moment, Tomás only thinks that these things are gone.

   D. This is the correct answer. It is Tomás's problem. He doesn't realize it at first, though.

As you read this passage, think about the main character's problem and how it is solved.

Mom and I had always lived in the old apartment house at 311 West Street. It was home, even if it was run-down. Years ago, we had put our names on a list to get a place in some garden apartments the city was building on the other side of the city. I had forgotten all about that. So I was surprised when I got home from school last Friday to see Mom waving an official-looking letter. "Guess what, Sung!" she called. "The new apartment just came through!"

"That's great, Mom!" I said. But was it really? As I walked over to tell Bo, I began to think about the neighborhood where I had always lived. There was the Lark Street pool and the playground and the school and all my friends. I didn't want to leave any of them.

"So you won't be able to play ball with the Comets," Bo said **morosely**. He sure wasn't happy to hear the news.

"I went to see the new apartment after work," Mom told me when she got home today. "It's brand new but really small. It's really far from the stores and the new school you'd go to, and I'd have to take two buses to get to work." "So," she continued, "if it's all right with you, I've sort of decided not to take it."

"All right?" I said. "That's great!"

1. Ⓐ Ⓑ Ⓒ Ⓓ
2. Ⓐ Ⓑ Ⓒ Ⓓ
3. Ⓐ Ⓑ Ⓒ Ⓓ

Mark the best answer for questions 1–3.

1. What is the main problem in this story?

    A. Sung's new apartment is too far from the school.

    B. Sung doesn't want to move.

    C. Sung's apartment is run-down.

    D. Sung's Mom can't find a new place.

2. The solution comes when

    A. Sung walks over to Bo.

    B. Sung visits his new school.

    C. a new apartment becomes available.

    D. Sung's mother decides not to move.

3. The word **morosely** in paragraph 3 means

    A. foolishly.

    B. sadly.

    C. happily.

    D. unfairly.

4. Do you think Sung and his mother have made the right decision? Write two sentences to explain your answer.

_____

_____

_____

_____

Setting

The **setting** is the **time** and the **place** in which the action of a story takes place. The setting might be a Western ranch in 1885, the planet Mars in 2450, or your own living room this afternoon. Often the author states where and when the story takes place. At other times, you have to figure out the setting from details scattered through the text.

A story's setting can affect the characters and plot. Characters forced to spend the night in an old abandoned house during a thunderstorm, for example, might become terrified and do something foolish. In a story set in a remote area before the invention of the automobile, a medical problem might become a life-threatening emergency.

Tips for Success
- Remember that the setting includes both the time and the place.
- The setting often affects the characters or the events of the plot.

As you read this passage, think about its setting—where and when the story takes place.

Magda stared sadly at the broken chain on her bicycle. It certainly had chosen an inconvenient time to snap. Now what should she do? A few miles back, she had passed the little town of Mineville. Would anyone there be able to fix her bicycle?

The January sun was setting fast, and a snowy wind whistled through the pines. Magda shivered. Bicycling over the mountains to Aunt Felicia's had seemed like such a good idea that afternoon.

Pushing her bike, Magda trudged up the next hill and down the other side. As it grew darker, snow began to fall. Magda sighed. There were six or seven miles of nothing between here and Aunt Felicia's cabin in Dowager.

Suddenly a pair of headlights swept over the hilltop and three honks broke the darkness. "When you didn't arrive at the cabin, I thought you might have had a problem," Aunt Felicia called out. "So I came out to find you."

1. What is the setting of this story?
   A. Aunt Felicia's cabin in Dowager late at night
   B. a deserted mountain road late on a winter day
   C. the small town of Mineville near noon on a January day
   D. a desert region during a summer mountain biking trip

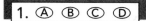
1. Ⓐ Ⓑ Ⓒ Ⓓ

Mark your answer choice by filling in the oval.

✔ **Now check to see whether you chose the correct answer.**

   A. The story mentions this cabin, but the action isn't set there.
   B. This is the correct answer. The story describes Magda on a mountain road at sundown on a January night.
   C. Magda recalls passing through this town, but no action is set there.
   D. None of the details in the passage describe this setting.

As you read this passage, think about its setting.

When Mona arrived at V-Dome 7, she hadn't known that each night on the planet lasted 58 Earth days. For someone who loved sunshine, that was difficult to take. Now, though, the sun had finally risen, and it would shine for 58 days. Not that the sun was ever bright enough. "Looks like a foggy winter afternoon in San Francisco," announced Mona, staring at the peach-colored planet. "Still, I think I'll go out for a walk."

Tracy glanced nervously at her friend. A walk? Dome dwellers didn't go out for walks. Not when the temperature is 465°C, and the air pressure—mainly carbon dioxide—crushes you in a second. No one went outside the dome, except in a fully pressurized V-Ranger with oxygen support. Did Mona have Dome Syndrome, the inability to adjust to life inside a huge glass dome?

"Yes, I'll hike to the T74 Hills," Mona continued. "I'm convinced some Venusians still live there."

Venusians! Tracy's eyes widened. Only last year, Robert had talked of Venusians. That was just before he broke security and opened a dome door to go swimming with them! How many dome dwellers died in that disaster? Smiling at her friend, Tracy used her mind pager to alert Psychological Services. They'd have to reprogram Mona's emotions in time to save her.

---

1. Ⓐ Ⓑ Ⓒ Ⓓ
2. Ⓐ Ⓑ Ⓒ Ⓓ
3. Ⓐ Ⓑ Ⓒ Ⓓ
4. Ⓐ Ⓑ Ⓒ Ⓓ

Mark the best answer for questions 1–4.

1. Where does the action in this story take place?

   A. near San Francisco

   B. in a spacecraft in space

   C. on a star far from our galaxy

   D. in a space colony on Venus

2. The action probably takes place

   A. in the 1960s, during the early days of the space program.

   B. at the present time.

   C. a few years from now.

   D. in the distant future.

3. As the passage opens, why is Mona uncomfortable with the setting?

   A. The temperature is too hot.

   B. The sun doesn't shine brightly.

   C. The landscape is peach-colored.

   D. The air is not fresh.

4. The author suggests that the setting causes some people

   A. to become violent.

   B. to become more self-reliant.

   C. to imagine things.

   D. to appreciate others more.

5. Explain why Mona wouldn't be able to take a walk outside V-Dome 7.

   _____

   _____

   _____

Lesson 4 Theme

The **theme** is the main idea or message that the author wants you to get from the story. Usually an author doesn't state the theme directly. Instead, the author uses the other elements of a story—plot, characters, and setting—to develop the theme. You can figure out the theme by paying attention to what happens to the characters as the plot unfolds.

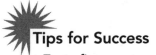

Tips for Success

- Try to figure out the message the author wants to get across.
- Decide which answer choice best sums up the main idea of the story.

As you read this fable, think about its main idea, or theme.

Long ago, the different parts of the body didn't always work together as well as they do today. Besides fighting among themselves, Head, Legs, and Arms never got along very well with Belly. They thought he was lazy since all he ever did was enjoy his food.

One day, Head decided to teach Belly a lesson. "I'm not thinking up ways to find food anymore!" he said.

"Good plan," agreed Legs. "I won't bother to walk over to any food either."

"Right," said Arms, "and I won't pick it up. We'll show that lazy Belly."

After a few weeks with no food, Belly was really grumbling, but the other body parts had problems, too. Head was dizzy, Legs was too weak to walk, and Arms was covered with sores.

Head called a meeting. "As useless as Belly seems to be," he said, "he must have a purpose or we wouldn't be feeling so sick." Arms and Legs agreed, so they all decided to go out and find something to eat right away.

1. What is the theme of this story?

    A. Sometimes it's necessary to teach someone a lesson.

    B. Everyone has a role to play in working for the common good.

    C. It's important to eat three healthful meals a day.

    D. Some people are unhappy no matter what you do.

1. Ⓐ Ⓑ Ⓒ Ⓓ

Mark your answer choice by filling in the oval.

✓ **Now check to see whether you chose the correct answer.**

    A. The body parts did try to teach Belly a lesson, but it didn't work as planned. However, this is not the main idea of the fable.

    B. This is the correct answer. It is the main idea, or theme. The body parts realize that Belly has a role to play for their common good.

    C. While eating is important in the tale, this is not the author's main message.

    D. The characters and plot events do not develop this idea.

This passage is set in France during World War II. Determine the theme by thinking about how the characters act.

Ever since the Germans had occupied their homeland, the rumble of trucks through St. Barre seemed endless. "What are they carrying anyway?" asked Claude, walking home from school with Danielle.

"Ammunition. They're taking it to the **front** to resupply their soldiers," Danielle explained. Then she glanced over at him slyly. "How would you like to slow them down?"

Claude watched the huge green trucks approach, so heavy they seemed to crush the asphalt. "Me? Stop them? There's no way."

"Here's a way," said Danielle, pulling a paper bag from her pack. It was full of nails with broad, flat heads. She motioned to Claude to crouch down behind the stone wall high above the road. Then she begin tossing the nails onto the roadbed.

The two of them tossed nails until the enemy trucks were just a hundred meters away. Then, ducking down, they waited. Blam! The exploding tire sounded like a gunshot. Then again, Blam! "Two blowouts!" whispered Danielle excitedly. "Those trucks are so heavy it will take them all afternoon to change those tires!"

Silently, Danielle and Claude crept away. "It was the nails I threw that stopped the Germans," claimed Claude. "I'm sure of it."

---

1. Ⓐ Ⓑ Ⓒ Ⓓ
2. Ⓐ Ⓑ Ⓒ Ⓓ
3. Ⓐ Ⓑ Ⓒ Ⓓ

Mark the best answer for questions 1–3.

1. What is one main idea of this story?
   A. War forces people to do strange things.
   B. People are cowards when those around them are brave.
   C. It's foolish to fight a powerful foe.
   D. The small can defeat the powerful.

2. Another message of this story is:
   A. Ordinary people face hardships in wartime.
   B. Children's games can be destructive.
   C. There are many ways to fight a foe.
   D. Good people are often hated.

3. The word **front** in paragraph 2 means
   A. the most important side.
   B. the part ahead of the rest.
   C. a person or thing used as a cover to hide something else.
   D. the place where a battle is fought.

4. Describe the theme of the story in your own words.

_____

_____

_____

In these pages, you can use the skills you have practiced in this chapter. Read the story and answer the questions. Mark your answer choices by filling in the ovals.

A Voice in the Darkness

1. Colonel Henry Ludington stacked the last sacks of flour and straightened his back with a groan. Time to close the mill and eat supper. The day had been a busy one, and he wasn't as young as he used to be. The bullet he had taken in the shoulder back in '54 during the French and Indian War bothered him more each year. Now it seemed another war was brewing. Ludington shook his head at the thought. As leader of the local New York militia, he must soon call his men together. They needed to be drilled and equipped when the trouble came.

2. Hoofbeats from the road broke into the miller's thoughts. From the way the rider was lying against his horse's neck, Ludington could see that something was very wrong. "Are you hurt?" Ludington called, hurrying out to grab the horse's bridle.

3. "British soldiers—they put a bullet in me," the man groaned, "but I got away. They've landed at Compo Beach and they're burning Danbury. Help us, Colonel. We gotta have help." With that, the rider slid unconscious to the ground.

4. The British were in Connecticut, just 40 miles away! Ludington had to assemble the men at once. But he couldn't ride to get them himself. He had to be at the mill to make sure they were organized and equipped. He'd need a messenger who knew each farm and country road for miles around. The messenger would need to rouse the men so they'd be at the mill and ready to march with him at daybreak.

5. "What's happened, Pa? Where did he come from? Should I get Ma?" Ludington's daughter Sybil suddenly stood beside him. Her blue eyes were wide as she stared at the wounded man. She rolled her hands inside her apron, a sign that she was worried.

6. "He comes from Danbury. The British are burning the place, and yes, get your mother," said the Colonel. As the Ludingtons moved the man onto a cot in the mill, the Colonel quickly explained his **predicament** to his wife and daughter. "Should I go call the men together or stay here and organize them?"

7. "I'll go on Prince, Pa," Sybil volunteered. "We both know the roads. Please! I'll ride straight down to McKiel's Corners and then circle back over the Pawling Road to go by all the farms. I'll come out by Riddle's and then up the Post Road." Like a shot, Sybil was off for the house before her father could reply.

8. "Sybil, that's out of the question!" Mrs. Ludington shouted at her retreating daughter. "A girl riding all night through woods filled with bandits and riffraff! I won't have it!"

9. "You're right, Mary, of course," agreed the Colonel, torn between duty to his country and his love for his daughter. "A girl like Sybil should not go. But who can I send?"

10. As if in answer, Sybil galloped down the mill lane on Prince. "Sybil, no!" screamed Mrs. Ludington. "No!" But her daughter was already on the pike, galloping away in the fast-fading sunlight.

11. As Prince thundered east, Sybil reviewed her route. She must cover the Putnam County settlements first and then work southwest back to the river. The ride—forty or fifty miles at least— would take all night. She reined in Prince to a trot so he wouldn't tire too early.

12. All night long, Sybil hurried down the muddy roads through villages and farms. All night long, she carried the message to her father's men. And alone or in groups of two or three, they made their way to Ludington's Mill to join in the fight for independence.

13. All went well until after midnight when Sybil took the shortcut from the river up to the Post Road. At least she thought it was the shortcut. In the darkness, she couldn't be sure. Prince was exhausted and panting hard, stumbling now and then in the rutted

trail. Suddenly, just ahead, Sybil spotted the flash of a lantern. "Who goes there?" a harsh voice cried.

14. Sybil's pounding heart shook her body. Prince was scared, too, for his big frame quivered under her. Up ahead, several shadowy figures now blocked the path. Would they try to **check** her passage? Knowing it was too late to turn around and somehow sensing she must not stop, Sybil struck Prince with her heels and charged. In answer, Prince tensed every muscle and lunged forward at the men. They scattered like dry leaves in a wind, their angry cries still echoing in the dark when Sybil got to the Post Road.

15. It was gray dawn when the mill came into view. Prince had slowed to a walk, his black sides heaving. Men were marching in the distance—many men—and Sybil heard her father shouting sharp, quick orders. As she drew nearer, the men gathered around her, cheering, "Hurray for Sybil Ludington! Hurray for the Colonel's girl!" Sitting up proudly in her saddle, Sybil waved and grinned at the militia men as they marched away. They were off to join General Sullivan and his army, off to defeat the British at Ridgefield, and off to take their place in history.

SETTING

1. This story takes place over a period of about
   A. two hours.
   B. 12 hours.
   C. two or three days.
   D. a week.

CHARACTER

2. Based on how she became her father's messenger, you can tell Sybil was
   A. obedient.
   B. independent.
   C. nervous.
   D. selfish.

1. Ⓐ Ⓑ Ⓒ Ⓓ
2. Ⓐ Ⓑ Ⓒ Ⓓ

3. Ⓐ Ⓑ Ⓒ Ⓓ
4. Ⓐ Ⓑ Ⓒ Ⓓ
5. Ⓐ Ⓑ Ⓒ Ⓓ
6. Ⓐ Ⓑ Ⓒ Ⓓ
7. Ⓐ Ⓑ Ⓒ Ⓓ
8. Ⓐ Ⓑ Ⓒ Ⓓ

PLOT

3. What is the main problem that Colonel Ludington faces in the story?

A. He is not in good enough health to lead his men.

B. His men lack the equipment and willingness to fight.

C. He can't call his men together and organize them at the same time.

D. He isn't sure where the Americans are to meet the British in battle.

PLOT

4. Why doesn't Mr. Ludington want Sybil to ride out to warn his men?

A. He knows that this is his responsibility as colonel of the militia.

B. He needs Sybil to look after the wounded man.

C. He doesn't think Sybil will be able to ride fast enough at night.

D. He feels the task is too dangerous.

SETTING

5. The action of the story begins

A. in Danbury and ends in Ridgefield.

B. at Ludington's Mill and ends in the woods by the river.

C. and ends at Ludington's Mill.

D. in Danbury and ends at Ludington's Mill.

PLOT

6. The main problem that Sybil faces on her ride occurs when

A. several strangers try to stop her on a shortcut through the woods.

B. members of the militia don't believe the British have burned Danbury.

C. she keeps getting lost on the dark roads and trails.

D. her horse Prince tires and refuses to continue on.

VOCABULARY

7. The word **predicament** in paragraph 6 means

A. solution.

B. misgivings.

C. problem.

D. relief.

CHARACTER

8. At the end of the story, Sybil seems to feel

A. frightened, because a war is about to begin.

B. happy, because she has completed her mission successfully.

C. afraid, because she knows her parents didn't want her to ride out and warn the men.

D. exhausted, because she has narrowly escaped disaster.

9. In paragraph 14, what does the word **check** mean?

   A. to prove to be right

   B. to mark with a check

   C. to stop suddenly

   D. to put in a special place for a time

THEME

10. Which of these sentences states a theme of the story?

    A. Attempting to do more than you're capable of can cause a disaster.

    B. In emergencies, people must take bold measures.

    C. It's a lot easier to imagine yourself a hero than to do heroic things.

    D. The true cost of warfare is greater than people realize.

THEME

11. Which message does the author PROBABLY want readers to learn from this story?

    A. People of the past had much harder lives than people do today.

    B. At the beginning of the Revolution, the Americans were a well-trained fighting force.

    C. Women and young people played an important role in securing our nation's independence.

    D. Few people are fully prepared to serve their country when the need arises.

9.	Ⓐ Ⓑ Ⓒ Ⓓ
10.	Ⓐ Ⓑ Ⓒ Ⓓ
11.	Ⓐ Ⓑ Ⓒ Ⓓ

12. This story is set in 1775, at the very beginning of the American Revolution. Tell how you think this setting affects Sybil as she goes about her task.

_____

_____

_____

_____

13. Think about the title of this story—"A Voice in the Darkness." Why do you think the author chose this title?

_____

_____

_____

_____

STOP

CHAPTER 2 Informational Text

Most of what you read in school is **informational text**. This important type of writing is always part of formal reading tests, too. Here are some common questions about informational text.

 What is an informational text?
Anything that was written mainly to give information about a topic is an informational text.

 What types of reading materials are informational texts?
The informational texts you're probably most familiar with are social studies and science textbooks. The articles in encyclopedias are also informational text. So are most newspaper and magazine articles.

 What are the major elements of informational text?
Informational texts have a central purpose, major ideas, and supporting details, and they often have visual aids such as maps, graphs, and tables. A book-length text may contain a table of contents and an index.

- The **central purpose** is what the author is most interested in telling you. It's what the author wants to accomplish by writing the text.

- A **major idea** is the important point made in a section of informational text. Sometimes it is called the **main idea**. The **supporting details** in an informational text develop and explain the major ideas.

- Graphs, maps, and tables are **visual aids** that organize a great deal of information in an easy-to-use form.

- A **table of contents** appears at the beginning of a book and lists the chapters or other parts of the book and the pages on which they begin. An **index** appears at the end of a book. It is an alphabetical list of topics in the book and the pages on which they are mentioned.

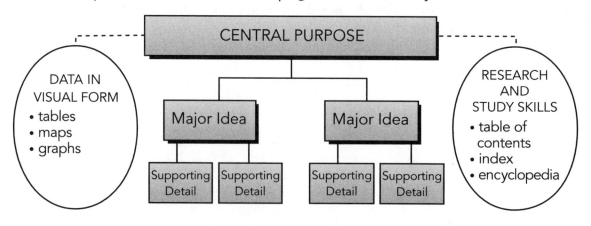

Test Questions About Informational Text

Most test questions about informational text focus on central purpose, major ideas, and supporting details. The test may also ask questions about a table of contents, an index, or a graph. Questions about informational text take many different forms. The questions below come from actual tests and show the most common types of questions.

Questions About Central Purpose

- What is the central purpose of this article?
- What was the author trying to accomplish by writing this selection?
- The author feels that it is very important for people to _____.

Questions About Major Ideas

- What is the main idea of this passage?
- Which feature MOST helps the camel survive in the desert?
- Why did starlings spread so rapidly in the United States?

Questions About Supporting Details

- Where did most pioneers begin the journey West?
- Which of the following supported the moon landing?
- Why did scientists name Mars after the Roman god of war?

Questions About Tables, Graphs, and Maps

- In what year did Woodrow Wilson become President?
- With which states does Kansas share a border?
- What was the population of Canada in 1920?
- What percentage of their income do the Petersons spend on rent?
- Which country has the largest area?
- How long is the Erie Canal?

Questions About Tables of Contents and Indexes

- On which page does Part IV begin?
- Which chapter tells about the growth of railroads?
- Which pages tell about Canadian-style football?
- Where might you look to find the effects of alcohol on the brain?

The lessons in Chapter 2 will help you understand how to answer test questions about central purpose, major ideas, and supporting details in informational text. You'll read some short passages and answer a few questions. The upcoming lessons will also help you work with visual aids, tables of contents, and indexes.

Central Purpose

Reading tests often ask you about the **central purpose** of an informational article. The central purpose is the focus of the entire selection. This is what the author most wants you to learn.

The central purpose of an article about monarch butterflies, for example, might be to describe their migration routes. The central purpose of a piece about national parks could be to state that many parks are being overused.

To find the central purpose, think about the different facts mentioned in an informational article. Usually they work together to present the central purpose.

Tips for Success

- Ask yourself what the author most wants you to learn.
- Remember that a selection will contain many true statements that are not the central purpose.
- The central purpose is likely to be a general statement concerning the entire selection.

Read this passage about electric cars. Decide what the author most wants you to learn.

They're quiet, kind to the environment, and have a twenty-first-century flair. Even so, electric cars aren't likely to be seen on Main Street, USA, anytime soon. One reason is cost. So few EV's (electric vehicles) are made each year that even a tiny one costs more than a giant gas guzzler. The EV's short range is another problem. The batteries of these cars have to be recharged every 100 miles or so. That's inconvenient on a long trip, especially since finding places to recharge isn't easy.

1. The central purpose of this passage is
   A. to explain that electric cars are quiet, good for the environment, and modern-looking.
   B. to tell you that right now the drawbacks of EV's outweigh their benefits.
   C. to tell you that the recharging of electric cars is a major problem for motorists.
   D. to let you know that EV's are quite expensive.

1. Ⓐ Ⓑ Ⓒ Ⓓ

Mark your answer choice by filling in the oval.

✔ **Now check to see whether you chose the correct answer.**

   A. Telling about these advantages is not the central purpose.
   B. This is the correct answer. All the facts in the passage work together to express this central idea.
   C. This is true, but it's not the main focus of the article.
   D. While the author tells you this, it's not what he or she most wants you to learn.

As you read each passage, think about its central purpose.

One of the newest environmental challenges facing America is an inch-long, black-and-white striped shellfish. Accidentally carried to the Great Lakes by a tanker in 1985, zebra mussels are spreading to every state. Why is that a problem? For one thing, the mussels reproduce quickly and have no enemies. Worse, they form dense colonies that clog water mains and factory cooling systems. Zebra mussels also interfere with shipping and make a mess along the shorelines. Cities now expend millions to undo the damage, but the problem grows worse. The zebra mussels also eat so many tiny water plants that it's hard for some fish to survive.

One of the most famous tombs in the world was discovered in 1974 in Xian, China. Workers there unearthed a huge burial pit guarded by a 4,000-year-old clay army. Covering several square miles, the tomb contains 7,000 life-sized warriors, 600 clay horses, and 130 chariots. The figures, each with detailed faces, are arranged in battle formation. The tomb was built for Shi Huang Di, the first emperor of China. A ruthless leader, Shi Huang Di unified China by taxing people and forcing them to do unpaid labor. This created many enemies for the emperor. Perhaps that's why he needed an army to protect him, even after he died!

1. Ⓐ Ⓑ Ⓒ Ⓓ
2. Ⓐ Ⓑ Ⓒ Ⓓ

Mark the best answer for questions 1–2.

1. What idea does the author of the first passage MOST want to express?

   A. America has many environmental challenges.

   B. Zebra mussels clog water mains and factory cooling systems.

   C. Zebra mussels might cause certain types of fish to die out.

   D. Zebra mussels are causing a serious environmental problem.

2. The author of the second passage makes the central point that

   A. the first emperor of China liked to play with clay warriors.

   B. the Xian tomb contains 7,000 clay warriors, horses, and chariots.

   C. the first Chinese emperor's tomb was guarded by a huge clay army.

   D. an amazing tomb was found in China in 1975.

3. Pick a passage from above. What does the author most want you to learn?

_____

_____

_____

Lesson 2 # Major Ideas

Major ideas are the most important points made within a paragraph or section of a longer selection. Sometimes an author states a major idea directly. Sometimes you have to figure it out from the details. To decide on the major idea, ask yourself what the section is about. Often the major idea is a general statement that sums up the section.

When you're choosing your answer on a test, don't be fooled by statements that are from the passage and seem to be true. Remember that the correct answer will tell the most important information.

⭐ **Tips for Success**

• **Think about the most important point within a paragraph or section of a selection.**

• **Don't just pick any true statement from a passage as your answer. Check to see that your choice answers the question.**

As you read this passage, look for the major idea.

Back in 1924, the last native condors in Arizona disappeared. In 1998, however, 25 of the black-feathered, orange-headed giants began trying out their 10-foot wingspans there. The new Arizonan condors had been hatched, bred, and released by wildlife biologists. All of the birds were just two years old. The biologists equipped the condors with small radio transmitters to follow the birds' movements. In general, the biologists were thrilled that the condors were doing so well. Learning to survive in the wild without the training of natural parents is never easy. The program to breed and release condors had succeeded.

1. What is the major idea of the passage?

   A. Back in 1924, the last native condors disappeared in Arizona.

   B. Biologists equipped condors with small radio transmitters to follow their movements.

   C. Biologists bred and released young condors in Arizona.

   D. Learning to survive in the wild without the training of natural parents is never easy.

1. Ⓐ Ⓑ Ⓒ Ⓓ   **Mark your answer choice by filling in the oval.**

✓ **Now check to see whether you chose the correct answer.**

   A. This fact is mentioned in the passage, but it's not the most important idea.

   B. This isn't the most important point.

   C. This is the correct answer. It is the most important idea in the passage, because biologists were instrumental in bringing back the condor to Arizona.

   D. This statement may be true, but it isn't the main idea.

As you read these passages taken from longer articles, think about their major ideas.

Polytetrafluoroethylene is amazing stuff. Heat and cold don't affect it. Acid doesn't attack it. Plus, it's so slippery that nothing sticks to it. Such a handy material needed an easier name. So chemist Roy Plunkett called it Teflon. He discovered the plastic by accident in 1938. While working with gases used to keep refrigerators cold, Plunkett left some Freon gas in cold storage overnight. By morning, the gas had changed into a solid white powder with amazing properties. At first, Teflon was used by atomic bomb scientists to contain uranium. By the 1960s, companies were spreading the stick-free coating on pots and pans. The plastic is so versatile that it can even be stretched into a water-resistant, breathable fabric.

The Internet is the world's largest computer network. Set up in 1970 as Arpenet, the system linked only a few scientists in the defense industry. Arpenet grew slowly, expanding to about 1,000 computers by 1984. The scientists found the network very helpful for their work. In time, other researchers decided they needed a computer network, too. So the system expanded. By 1989, the network served 100,000 computers. In 1992, the system, now called "the Internet," linked one million computers. The following year it was two million. Ordinary citizens had decided the network had a lot to offer them, too. Today the total number of computers linked by the Internet is anybody's guess.

1. Ⓐ Ⓑ Ⓒ Ⓓ
2. Ⓐ Ⓑ Ⓒ Ⓓ

Mark the best answer for questions 1–2.

1. Why is Teflon such amazing stuff?

   A. It was discovered by accident.

   B. Chemist Roy Plunkett made Teflon in 1938 while working with Freon gas.

   C. Teflon is stick-free and unaffected by heat, cold, or acid.

   D. Teflon can be stretched into a water-resistant fabric.

2. What is the major idea in this passage about the Internet?

   A. The Internet was set up in 1970.

   B. At first, only scientists in the defense industry used the computer network.

   C. Set up as a small network, the Internet has grown rapidly.

   D. No one knows how many computers are linked by the Internet.

3. In your own words, explain why the Internet grew so rapidly.

_____

_____

_____

Lesson 3 Supporting Details

Supporting details are the details in a passage that support, or tell more about, the major ideas. These details are often facts, examples, or quotations. Authors include supporting details to help you understand the major ideas in a piece of writing.

Suppose, for example, an author wrote a piece about how rare *T. rex* fossils are. The author might say that a museum paid $15 million for a *T. rex* fossil recently. Or, the author might explain that fewer than 100 *T. rex* skeletons have ever been found. These details support the major idea that the dinosaur fossils are very rare.

Tips for Success

- Make sure the answer you choose is a detail mentioned in the selection.
- Read the questions carefully. Don't be tricked into choosing details that don't answer the questions.

As you read this passage, look for details that support the main idea.

Throughout human history, smallpox has killed millions of people. In 1979, the disease of smallpox was finally eliminated from the Earth. Smallpox vaccinations, or shots, had been given since 1777, but there was no practical way to vaccinate everyone. So smallpox continued to kill. In the late 1950s, doctors began a containment policy. Instead of vaccinating everyone, they waited until smallpox broke out. Then they rushed to the site and gave shots to anyone who had been exposed to the virus. Containment wiped out smallpox in 20 African nations in the 1960s. By 1977, the policy had ended smallpox in India and Somalia, its last strongholds. Today the only smallpox virus left in the world is kept frozen in a government lab.

1. Based on the details in the passage, who was vaccinated under the smallpox containment policy?
   A. everyone in a country
   B. everyone with smallpox
   C. everyone exposed to the virus
   D. everyone who asked to be vaccinated

1. Ⓐ Ⓑ Ⓒ Ⓓ

Mark your answer choice by filling in the oval.

✔ **Now check to see whether you chose the correct answer.**

A. The selection says there was no practical way to vaccinate everyone.
B. There is nothing in the passage about vaccinating people who already had smallpox.
C. This is the correct answer. By vaccinating people exposed to the virus, the disease was contained.
D. There is nothing in the selection about people asking to be vaccinated.

Read the passage. Then answer the questions that follow.

Joe Redington loved Alaska and wanted to celebrate its heritage. So in 1973, he organized a 1,000-mile dogsled race called the Iditarod. At the time, few people thought the race would become successful. Only a few dogsleds took part the first few years.

In 1997, Alaskans enjoyed their 25th Iditarod. Now the race is a permanent part of Alaska's culture. Dozens of big companies sponsor the event. Hundreds of entrants come from all over the world. They compete for a $50,000 first prize. Thousands of Alaskans help organize the race and cheer the teams.

The race course follows winter paths first used by Native Americans. Miners used the same routes in the Gold Rush of 1900. The race also travels a route taken in 1925 when dogsledders rushed medicine to Nome, Alaska, to prevent an outbreak of disease.

The sled drivers, or mushers, face subzero temperatures, blinding storms, and avalanches. The race itself, however, faces an obstacle, too. Many people complain it is too hard on the dogs. Almost every year, one or more dogs die on the trail. As a result, some sponsors no longer support the race. The Iditarod organizers now make dog health an important concern. More vets are involved in the race, and mushers whose dogs die face **stiff** fines.

1. Ⓐ Ⓑ Ⓒ Ⓓ
2. Ⓐ Ⓑ Ⓒ Ⓓ
3. Ⓐ Ⓑ Ⓒ Ⓓ

Mark the best answer for questions 1–3.

1. According to the article, which is an obstacle facing the Iditarod today?

   A. Sponsors are upset that dogs often die during the race.

   B. Alaskans do not support the race.

   C. Sled drivers are injured in the subzero temperatures and snowstorms.

   D. Only a few sled drivers sign up.

2. What reason is given for why the Iditarod Race was begun?

   A. to honor the Native Americans who first lived in Alaska

   B. to bring medicine to Nome

   C. to preserve dogsledding before it disappeared

   D. to celebrate Alaska's heritage

3. What does the word **stiff** in the last paragraph mean?

   A. not able to move easily

   B. not relaxed; tense or formal

   C. harsh or severe

   D. powerful

4. What is the main idea of the passage? Write the main idea and then list two or three details that support it.

_____

_____

_____

Lesson 4 — Data in Visual Form

Many informational texts include tables, graphs, and maps. These **visual aids** contain a great deal of information that is clearly organized and easy to read. By using these visuals, you can find information quickly. Some of the informational text passages on reading tests often include visual aids to see how well you can locate specific data shown on these visual aids.

USING A TABLE

A **table** is an arrangement of facts in rows and columns. Each row and column has a label. By tracing the row and column until they meet, you can find the information you need.

Tips for Success

- Always read the titles of graphs, maps, and tables.
- Look carefully at the labels that appear on the side and bottom of a graph.
- Use a map's legend, scale, and compass to help you answer questions.
- Read "between the lines" of visual aids to draw conclusions.

Here is a table showing the populations of the South Asian countries.

COUNTRY				
Country	Capital City	Area (square miles)	Population (millions of people)	Population Doubling Time (years)
Bangladesh	Dhaka	50,260	113.9	29
Bhutan	Thimphu	18,150	1.4	30
India	New Delhi	1,147,950	897.4	34
Maldives	Malé	120	0.2	20
Nepal	Kathmandu	52,820	20.4	28
Pakistan	Islamabad	297,640	122.4	23
Sri Lanka	Colombo	24,950	17.8	49

Source: World Population Data Sheet of the Population Reference Bureau, Inc.

1. Which country in South Asia will double its population first?

   A. Bangladesh

   B. India

   C. Pakistan

   D. Maldives

1. Ⓐ Ⓑ Ⓒ Ⓓ

Mark your answer by filling in the oval.

✔ **Now check to see whether you chose the correct answer.**

   A. Bangladesh's population will double in 29 years. This is not the lowest number in the column "Population Doubling Time."

   B. India's population will double in 34 years.

   C. Pakistan's population will double in 23 years.

   D. This is the correct answer. Maldives's 20 years is the lowest number of all the countries.

Look back at the table on page 32 to answer questions 1–2.

1. The area of India is about
   A. twice the size of Pakistan.
   B. three times the size of Pakistan.
   C. four times the size of Pakistan.
   D. five times the size of Pakistan.

2. The population of India is about
   A. seven times that of Pakistan.
   B. six times that of Pakistan.
   C. five times that of Pakistan.
   D. the same as Pakistan.

USING A GRAPH

A **graph** shows numerical information visually. Graphs usually show how numbers or amounts vary by time or place. Graphs use lines, bars, or circles to show information. To read a line graph, pay attention to the **labels** along the bottom and up the side. Then check the **key** or **legend** to find out what each line represents.

Here is a graph that shows the percentage of populations in selected cities in Latin America during 1960–1990.

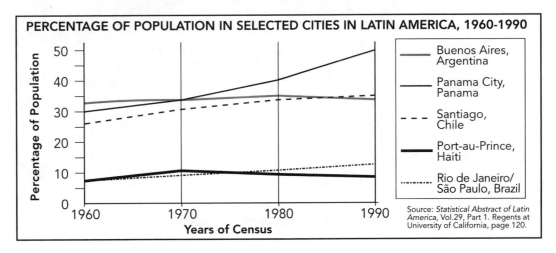

PERCENTAGE OF POPULATION IN SELECTED CITIES IN LATIN AMERICA, 1960-1990

Source: *Statistical Abstract of Latin America*, Vol.29, Part 1. Regents at University of California, page 120.

Use the graph to answer questions 3–4.

3. What percentage of Brazil's people lived in Rio de Janeiro/São Paulo in 1980?
   A. about 5 percent
   B. about 10 percent
   C. about 25 percent
   D. about 30 percent

4. Between 1970 and 1980, the percentage of Haiti's population in Port-au-Prince
   A. increased slightly.
   B. increased rapidly.
   C. decreased slightly.
   D. decreased rapidly.

USING A MAP

A **map** is a visual representation of a place. To find distances on a map, use the **scale**. To find out about specific locations, check the symbols that appear on the **legend**. The **compass** on the map shows directions.

Here is the map of the Han Empire during 210 B.C.–A.D. 220.

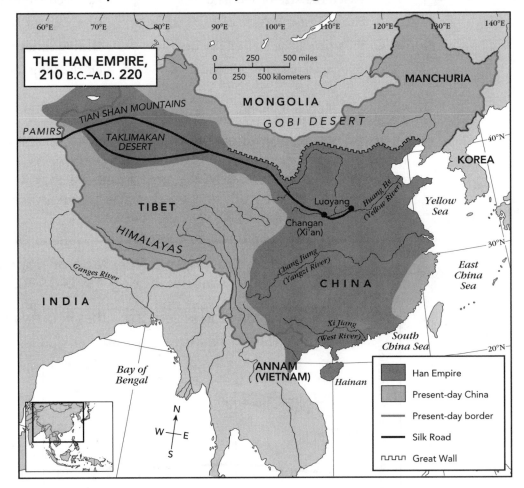

Use the map to answer questions 5–6.

5. Ⓐ Ⓑ Ⓒ Ⓓ
6. Ⓐ Ⓑ Ⓒ Ⓓ

5. How long is the Great Wall?

   A. about 750 miles

   B. about 1,500 miles

   C. about 2,500 miles

   D. over 4,000 miles

6. The Silk Road crossed

   A. Tibet and Mongolia.

   B. the Chang Jiang River.

   C. Manchuria.

   D. the Taklimakan Desert.

7. Contrast China's size during the Han Empire with its size today.

_____

_____

_____

Lesson 5 Research and Study Skills

Research and study skills are very important in understanding informational text. You often use specific parts of your textbooks, such as the table of contents and index. To find more about your topic, you also use other resources such as the encyclopedia.

USING A TABLE OF CONTENTS

A **table of contents** is located at the front of a book. It lists the contents of the book by chapter and page number. The table of contents provides you with a general outline of what is in the book.

Tips for Success
- The table of contents is not in alphabetical order. Use the chapter and section titles to search for the subject you want.
- Information on the same topic can appear in different places in a book.

Here is part of the table of contents from a U.S. history textbook.

Chapter 21	**The Great Crusade**	**438**
	The First World War	440
	Making the World Safe for Democracy	452
	The Search for a Lasting Peace	458
Chapter 22	**The Return to Normalcy**	**471**
	Conservatives in Control	473
	Americans Enjoy Prosperous Times	478
	The Economy Falters	485
Chapter 23	**Society and the Roaring Twenties**	**492**
	A Changing Society	494
	Patterns of Popular Culture	500
Chapter 24	**The Women's Rights Movement**	**512**
	The Role of Women Before the 1920s	514
	The Struggle for Suffrage	518
	The Nineteenth Amendment	526
	The Push for Equality Continues	530

1. Which chapter is MOST LIKELY to have information about Susan B. Anthony, who fought for women's voting rights?

A. Chapter 21

B. Chapter 22

C. Chapter 23

D. Chapter 24

1. Ⓐ Ⓑ Ⓒ Ⓓ

Mark your answer choice by filling in the oval.

Now check to see whether you chose the correct answer.

A. This chapter is mainly about World War I and its aftermath.

B. This chapter seems to be about the United States after World War I.

C. This chapter might mention women's rights, but it's not the best place.

D. This is the correct answer. The chapter about women's rights would be the most likely place to find information about Susan B. Anthony.

Look back at the table of contents on page 35 to answer questions 1–2.

1. (A) (B) (C) (D)
2. (A) (B) (C) (D)

1. Susan B. Anthony died before the amendment giving women the vote passed. Which section of Chapter 24 would be the BEST place to check for information about Susan B. Anthony?

   A. The Role of Women Before the 1920s

   B. The Struggle for Suffrage

   C. The Nineteenth Amendment

   D. The Push for Equality Continues

2. If you want to know whether women could own property and businesses in the early 1800s when Susan B. Anthony was born, on which pages would you be MOST LIKELY to find this information?

   A. 512–513

   B. 514–517

   C. 518–525

   D. 526–529

USING A BOOK INDEX

The **index** at the back of a book is an alphabetical listing of topics covered in the book. It lists all the pages in the book where each topic is mentioned. Using the index is a fast way to find information on a topic.

Here are some entries in the index for the U.S. history textbook.

> Amnesty Act of 1872, 335
> Annexation, 279, 385
> Anthony, Susan B., 419 *illus.*, 512, 514–516, 521, 587–588, 611
> Anthony Amendment, 591
> Antietam, 304
> Anti-Federalists, 127, 147
> Anti-Masons, 232

Use the index to answer questions 3–4.

3. (A) (B) (C) (D)
4. (A) (B) (C) (D)

3. On which page will you find a picture of Susan B. Anthony?

   A. 512

   B. 514–516

   C. 385

   D. 419

4. What information might be on page 591?

   A. information about annexation

   B. an illustration of Susan B. Anthony

   C. information about the Anthony Amendment

   D. information about Susan B. Anthony's life

USING AN ENCYCLOPEDIA INDEX

An **encyclopedia index** lists every reference to a topic in all the volumes of the encyclopedia. The index uses boldfaced type to list the letter of the volume and the page number where the article can be found.

Here are some entries from an encyclopedia index.

> **Anthony, Henry B.** [American political leader]
>   Kansas (table) **K:193**
> **Anthony, Susan Brownell** [American social reformer]
>   **A:508** *with portrait*
>   Civil Disobedience (History of Civil Disobedience) **C:465**
>   Dollar, picture on **D:244**
>   Woman Suffrage (Growth of the Movement) **W:322**
> *Anthony Adverse* [book by Allen]

Use the index entries to answer questions 5–6.

5. Ⓐ Ⓑ Ⓒ Ⓓ
6. Ⓐ Ⓑ Ⓒ Ⓓ

5. To learn about Susan B. Anthony being honored on United States currency, you should check
   A. Volume A, page 508.
   B. Volume C, page 465.
   C. Volume D, page 244.
   D. Volume W, page 322.

6. To find out whether Susan B. Anthony was on good terms with Elizabeth C. Stanton, another suffrage leader, you should check
   A. Volume A, page 508.
   B. Volume C, page 465.
   C. Volume D, page 244.
   D. Volume W, page 322.

7. If you were writing a research paper on Susan B. Anthony, how would using a table of contents, book index, and encyclopedia index help you?

_____

_____

_____

_____

_____

Informational Text

45 In these pages, you can use the skills you have practiced in this chapter. Read the passage and answer the questions. Mark your answer choices by filling in the ovals.

Relations with Latin America

1. After the United States won control of the Philippines in 1898, it decided to build a canal to link the Pacific with the Atlantic Ocean. Such an artificial waterway could be cut across Panama, in Central America. The canal would make the voyage from ocean to ocean thousands of miles shorter for trading and naval ships.

2. In 1901, President Theodore Roosevelt set plans for the canal in motion. At the time, Panama was a part of the Republic of Colombia. The United States offered Colombia's government $10 million for rights to the land. Colombia refused.

Panama Breaks Away

3. While Colombia hoped to get better terms by refusing, people in Panama did not want to lose the canal. Panamanian leaders decided to break away from Colombia and create a separate nation. President Roosevelt supported them. When Panamanians staged an uprising against Colombia, American warships kept Colombian ships from landing troops to put down the revolt. The United States then quickly decided to **recognize** an independent Panama.

4. The United States and Panama soon signed a canal treaty. For permanent rights to a canal zone 10 miles wide, the United States paid Panama $10 million. The United States also agreed to pay $250,000 rent to Panama every year.

5. For more than ten years, thousands of workers struggled to build the canal. They dynamited gorges in the jungles and built canal locks in 120-degree heat. Mudslides sometimes buried men and whole trains. The hot, steamy climate destroyed workers' health. Mosquitoes carried yellow fever

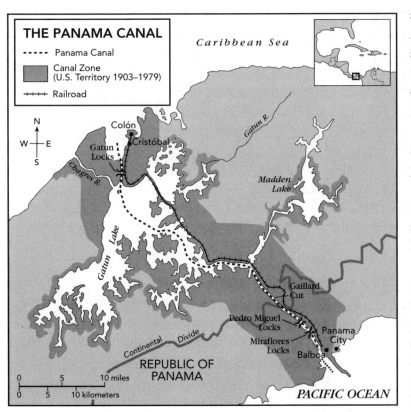

THE PANAMA CANAL

- - - - Panama Canal

Canal Zone (U.S. Territory 1903–1979)

++++ Railroad

Caribbean Sea

Colón
Cristóbal
Gatun Locks
Gatun R.
Chagres R.
Madden Lake
Gatun Lake
Gaillard Cut
Pedro Miguel Locks
Continental Divide
Miraflores Locks
Panama City
Balboa
REPUBLIC OF PANAMA

0   5   10 miles
0   5   10 kilometers

PACIFIC OCEAN

and malaria. Accidental dynamite blasts were another horror. Nevertheless, work went on until the canal was completed. In 1914, the Panama Canal finally opened to ships. To make up for the loss of Panama, the United States paid $425 million to Colombia in 1921.

U.S. Plays a Larger Role

6. With the construction of the Panama Canal, the United States began to play a larger role in Latin America. In 1823, the United States had issued the Monroe Doctrine, hoping to keep European nations from interfering in Latin American affairs. By 1900, European nations had lent large sums of money to Latin America. Some of these nations, including Venezuela and the Dominican Republic, had trouble paying their debts. So the Europeans threatened to use force to make them pay.

7. In 1904, President Roosevelt added the Roosevelt Corollary to the Monroe Doctrine. This corollary, or additional point, stated that the United States would exercise "international police power" in Latin America. The U.S. government would settle differences between Europe and Latin America. For example, U.S. officials would collect taxes to pay the foreign debts of the Dominican Republic. Latin Americans resented the United States acting as "police."

8. Roosevelt's successor, President William Howard Taft, encouraged U.S. banks and businesses to invest in Latin America. Taft hoped that such investments would help the United States influence Latin America in a peaceful way. This investment policy came to be called "dollar diplomacy."

9. Unfortunately, dollar diplomacy increased tensions between Latin America and the United States. U.S. citizens wanted their investments protected. In 1906, the United States sent troops to Cuba and set up a military government. In 1910, U.S. marines were sent to crush a revolt in Nicaragua, and soon U.S. troops were also occupying Haiti.

10. Civil war in Mexico led to further U.S. involvement in Latin America. The Mexican Revolution began in 1910. Taft's successor, President Woodrow Wilson, twice sent troops into Mexico after U.S. citizens had been threatened. The Mexicans protested these actions, and animosity toward the United States deepened.

11. When Franklin Roosevelt was inaugurated as President in 1933, he pledged to "dedicate this nation to the policy of the good neighbor." He wanted the United States to be a neighbor who "respects himself and, because he does, respects the rights of others." Roosevelt took steps to become Latin America's good neighbor. He removed U.S. troops from Nicaragua and Haiti. He pledged not to send troops into Latin America again. In addition, he made trade agreements with Latin America that would benefit both Latin American countries and the United States.

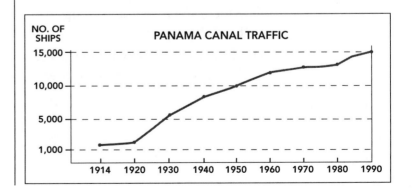

1. Ⓐ Ⓑ Ⓒ Ⓓ
2. Ⓐ Ⓑ Ⓒ Ⓓ
3. Ⓐ Ⓑ Ⓒ Ⓓ
4. Ⓐ Ⓑ Ⓒ Ⓓ
5. Ⓐ Ⓑ Ⓒ Ⓓ
6. Ⓐ Ⓑ Ⓒ Ⓓ

CENTRAL PURPOSE

1. The author's central purpose for writing this passage was to

A. show that canals are difficult to build.

B. prove that the U.S. has always been a good neighbor to Latin America.

C. tell about the U.S. role in Latin America.

D. explain the actions of different U.S. presidents in Latin America.

SUPPORTING DETAILS

2. Which detail supports the major idea of paragraph 5?

A. The United States paid Colombia $425 million in 1921.

B. The Panama Canal opened in 1914.

C. Mosquitoes in Panama carried yellow fever and malaria.

D. A canal lock raises or lowers a ship to another level.

MAJOR IDEA

3. Why did Franklin Roosevelt remove troops from Haiti and Nicaragua?

A. The Roosevelt Corollary demanded that he do so.

B. He wanted to trade more with these countries.

C. American citizens and troops had been threatened there.

D. He wanted to show more respect for the rights of these countries.

SUPPORTING DETAILS

4. Which example BEST shows "dollar diplomacy"?

A. The United States collected taxes in the Dominican Republic to pay that country's debts to Europe.

B. The United States paid $250,000 rent every year to Panama for rights to the canal.

C. American banks invested money in Latin America.

D. The United States declared itself the "police" in Latin America.

VOCABULARY

5. The meaning of **recognize** as used in paragraph 3 is

A. to give someone the right to speak at a meeting.

B. to become aware of something that has been seen.

C. to take notice of someone or something.

D. to accept as a new state or government.

MAP

6. Study the map on p. 38. To reach the Continental Divide from Balboa, a ship would travel

A. about 5 miles.

B. about 10 miles.

C. about 15 miles.

D. about 20 miles.

GRAPH

7. According to the graph on p. 39, how many ships passed through the Panama Canal in 1950?

A. 8,000

B. 10,000

C. 12,500

D. 15,000

GRAPH

8. How many more ships passed through the Panama Canal in 1990 than in 1940?

A. 7,000

B. 9,000

C. 14,000

D. 5,500

TABLE

9. The table below shows that Woodrow Wilson became president in

President	Term of Office	Political Party
William B. McKinley	1897-1901	Rep.
Theodore Roosevelt	1901-1909	Rep.
William Howard Taft	1909-1913	Rep.
Woodrow Wilson	1913-1921	Dem.
Calvin Coolidge	1923-1929	Rep.
Herbert C. Hoover	1929-1933	Rep.
Franklin D. Roosevelt	1933-1945	Dem.

A. 1909.

B. 1913.

C. 1921.

D. 1923.

TABLE OF CONTENTS

10. Which chapter would MOST LIKELY tell about Theodore Roosevelt's efforts to build the Panama Canal?

A. Chapter 25

B. Chapter 26

C. Chapter 27

D. Chapter 28

BOOK INDEX

11. On which pages are you LIKELY to find information about President Taft's efforts in Latin America?

A. 176

B. 181

C. 187, 189

D. 178

12. How did Franklin Roosevelt's attitude toward Latin America differ from that of earlier presidents?

_____

_____

_____

Persuasive text will also appear on most reading tests. Here are some common questions about persuasive text reading passages.

 What is a persuasive text?
Text that is persuasive tries to convince you to do or think something.

 What types of reading materials are persuasive texts?
Newspaper editorials are a common type of persuasive text that often appears on reading tests. Letters to the editor of a newspaper are usually persuasive, too. Advertisements in newspapers and magazines are another common type of persuasive text.

 What are the major elements of a persuasive text?
A persuasive text contains a main idea and supporting details. Usually a persuasive text uses facts and opinions to make its points. In addition, persuasive texts often compare and contrast ideas and information in an effort to influence readers.

- The **main idea** is the most important idea in a paragraph or passage of persuasive text. This is the main point the writer wants you to accept.

- The **supporting details** in a persuasive text develop and explain the main idea.

- A **fact** is a statement known to be true or something that can be checked or proven. An **opinion** is a statement that expresses a personal judgment, feeling, or belief. Opinions cannot be checked and proven to be true.

- To **compare** is to look for the ways in which things are similar or alike. To **contrast** is to look for the ways things differ.

All the elements of a persuasive text work together to convince you of something.

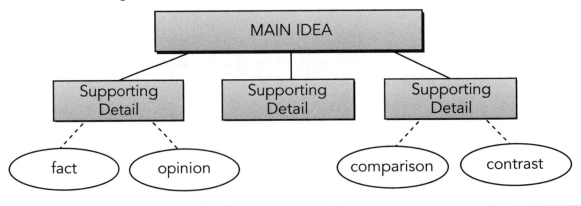

Test Questions About Persuasive Text

Many test questions about persuasive text focus on the main ideas that the author presents. You will also be asked about the details that are used to support main ideas. Other questions about persuasive text ask you to decide whether a statement is a fact or an opinion. The questions below come from actual tests. Studying them will help you become familiar with the most common types of questions about persuasive text.

Questions About Main Idea

- What does the writer of this editorial want the mayor to do?
- What position does the author take on school uniforms?
- Which statement BEST explains the main idea of this letter?
- What action would the writer of this letter NOT support?

Questions About Supporting Details

- Which of the following details supports the main idea of the letter?
- Which of these details do NOT support the author's main point?
- Why do you think the ad mentions Camp Cedar's new art program?
- Unemployment rose sharply during Governor Jones's last term. The editorial writer does not mention this because _____ .

Questions About Facts and Opinions

- Which of the following statements is a fact?
- Which of the following statements is an opinion?
- Which of the following statements cannot be proven?
- Which word in this statement suggests that it is an opinion?

Questions About Comparison and Contrast

- In which way is the Elm Street School like Barton Central School?
- Which statement BEST describes the difference between Rite-Ease and other athletic shoes?
- Which of the following statements reflects what Vista Hills offers but NOT Centerburg?
- Why does the writer compare education today to education 100 years ago?

The lessons in Chapter 3 will help you understand how to answer test questions about persuasive text. You'll read short passages of persuasive text that illustrate main idea and supporting details as well as facts and opinions. You'll also read pairs of passages on a similar topic to explore how comparisons and contrasts help to persuade.

Lesson 1 Main Idea

People who want to express their ideas tend to write persuasive text. In this type of writing—usually a letter or an editorial—there is usually one main idea. The **main idea** is the most important idea in a paragraph or passage. This is the main point the author wants you to accept.

The authors of persuasive text will try to make their main idea sound "right." That's because they want you to agree with them. As readers, however, it's important to think about these main ideas carefully before accepting them.

Tips for Success

• To understand the main point of a piece of persuasive writing, ask yourself what idea the writer wants you to accept.

• Watch out for information that is not backed up by the main idea.

As you read this letter to the editor, think about its main point.

To the Editor:

   With a silly new motto, "Dress for Success!" our school administrators lead the charge for a school uniform policy. I think "Dress for Conformity!" is more suitable. Wearing clothing with different colors and designs is a healthy way to express ourselves. Yet the school wants to force us all into light blue shirts, navy slacks, and plain white sneakers. This is a deliberate effort to crush our individuality. According to the newspaper, there's no real statewide proof that uniforms improve discipline or grades. Yet the principal claims uniforms will make students study harder and behave better. As far as I'm concerned, that's like believing in the tooth fairy.

Ed Campbell

1. What is the main idea of this letter?

   A. School uniforms do not improve students' grades according to a newspaper report.

   B. School officials are trying to crush the students' individuality.

   C. The drawbacks of the new school uniform program outweigh the supposed advantages of the program.

   D. "Dress for Success!" is a silly motto for the effort to make students wear school uniforms.

1. Ⓐ Ⓑ Ⓒ Ⓓ   **Mark your answer choice by filling in the oval.**

✔ **Now check to see whether you chose the correct answer.**

   A. This detail supports the writer's argument, but it is not the main point.

   B. The writer states this opinion, but again it is not the main idea.

   C. This is the correct answer. The statement sums up what the writer most wants the readers to accept.

   D. The writer opens the letter with this detail, but it is not the main point.

Don and Sara have written persuasive essays about getting weekly allowances. As you read each essay, think about its main point.

Don's Essay

By getting my $15 allowance every week, I know exactly how much money I'll have. That means I can budget my money—so much for video games, so much for treats, whatever. I also know that when I run out of money, I have myself to blame. That makes me more responsible the next week. An allowance also makes me feel independent. I don't have to nag my parents for money if I need something. I also have money on hand to take advantage of bargains. What's more, saving is easier with a regular allowance. I put $3 away every week to save for a mountain bike. By the way, my allowance isn't a hand-out. I have to do jobs around the house every week to get it. So allowances get me in the habit of working, too.

Sara's Essay

In the real world, no one gives you something for nothing. That's why it's better for kids to earn their money instead of getting an allowance. I know most kids say they do chores for their allowances; however, my friends get their hand-outs even when they forget to do their jobs. Having $15 or $20 handed to you each week doesn't teach responsibility either. It's not enough money to buy clothes or necessities. So most kids waste it on junk food or video games until they're broke. Then, if they really need money for something, they go to their parents for more. So much for responsibility! Last summer, I was a mother's helper. I earned $150 and felt a great deal of satisfaction. I saved half of it and spent the rest carefully, since I knew how hard it was to earn.

1. Ⓐ Ⓑ Ⓒ Ⓓ
2. Ⓐ Ⓑ Ⓒ Ⓓ

Mark the best answer for questions 1–2.

1. What is the main idea of Don's essay?

    A. Getting an allowance teaches kids to save money.

    B. Weekly allowances have benefits and drawbacks.

    C. Kids should be required to work for their weekly allowances.

    D. Kids learn to manage money wisely when they get allowances.

2. What is the main idea of Sara's essay?

    A. Kids who get an allowance will never learn to work hard.

    B. While some kids benefit from getting an allowance, others do not.

    C. Learning to handle money comes from working, not allowances.

    D. Most weekly allowances are too small to be meaningful.

3. Which essay is more persuasive to you? Use details to support your answer.

_____

_____

_____

Lesson 2 Supporting Details

Supporting details develop or tell more about the main idea of a passage. In persuasive text, writers include supporting details that will make their main ideas more appealing or persuasive. The details in a persuasive text help convince readers that the main idea is "right."

As readers, it's necessary to question whether the details in a persuasive text really support the main idea. It's also important to think about details that are *not* included. Often, a writer omits certain details because they argue against the main idea.

Tips for Success
- Figure out the main idea and then decide which details support it.
- Try to decide which details are most persuasive.

As you read this persuasive passage, think about its main idea and supporting details.

Television is great entertainment. Otherwise, the typical 18-year-old American would not have watched 19,000 hours of it. Television presents fine dramas and athletic events. TV news raises our awareness of the world. Unfortunately, television is also very violent. By age 18, the typical American has seen 200,000 acts of TV violence, including about 50,000 murders. In an 18-hour day, the average TV channel broadcasts 185 violent acts. Some people claim TV violence doesn't affect people. Nevertheless, violence is on the rise. According to one study, 80 percent of all Americans feel TV violence is making society more violent. If our communities are ever to be safe again, we must limit TV violence.

1. Which detail BEST supports the main idea of the passage?
   A. Television is wonderful entertainment.
   B. The typical American watches 19,000 hours of television by age 18.
   C. On a typical 18-hour day, the average TV channel broadcasts 185 violent acts.
   D. Some people claim TV violence doesn't affect people.

1. Ⓐ Ⓑ Ⓒ Ⓓ   **Mark your answer choice by filling in the oval.**

✔ **Now check to see whether you chose the correct answer.**

   A. The writer's main point deals with violence on television. This detail does not support it.
   B. This detail might support the main idea, but it's not the best supporting detail.
   C. This is the correct answer. This detail best supports the idea that TV violence is causing people to become more violent.
   D. This detail opposes the main idea of the passage.

This letter tries to persuade readers in Elmton that building an incinerator to burn garbage is a bad idea. As you read, think about the supporting details the writer uses.

To Elmton Residents:

Elmton will soon fill its landfill site and have no place for its garbage. To solve that problem, some residents want to build a garbage incinerator along the river. It doesn't make sense, in my opinion, to solve one problem by creating others.

For one thing, the incinerator would create pollution. The new plant would have filters to remove gases that pollute the air. However, many poisons are left in the ash. Incinerator ash has very high levels of lead and toxic metals. Put in our landfill, this poison could work its way into our drinking water! Paying to have it hauled away would cost a fortune and cause problems elsewhere.

State law now requires us to recycle newspaper, glass, and plastic. After we do that, we may not have the 2,000 tons of trash a week that the incinerator needs to run smoothly. Of course, Elmton could earn extra money by importing garbage from other cities. However, no one I know wants to do that. For that matter, no one that I know wants to build the incinerator!

Dena Furtado

---

1. Ⓐ Ⓑ Ⓒ Ⓓ
2. Ⓐ Ⓑ Ⓒ Ⓓ

Mark the best answer for questions 1–2.

1. Which detail BEST supports why Elmton should not build the incinerator?

   A. State law requires recycling of newspaper, glass, and plastic.

   B. The incinerator would have filters to remove gases that pollute the air.

   C. The toxic ash from the plant could poison people's water.

   D. The city might not have enough trash to keep the incinerator running.

2. Which detail does NOT support the main idea of the letter?

   A. Elmton could earn extra money by importing garbage from other cities.

   B. State law requires Elmton to recycle paper, glass, and plastic.

   C. Incinerator ash has very high levels of lead and toxic metals.

   D. No one that the writer knows wants to build the incinerator.

3. Which details support the idea that Ms. Furtado would probably agree with water conservation?

_____

_____

_____

Fact and Opinion

How can you judge the truth of the persuasive messages you hear every day? One way is to distinguish between fact and opinion.

- A **fact** is a statement known to be true or something that can be checked or proven. You can check factual information in reference books or other sources.

- An **opinion** is a statement that expresses a personal judgment, feeling, or belief. Opinions cannot be checked and proven to be true. Opinions often contain words such as *believe, best, better, worse, must, should,* and *probably*. Words like these express feelings and judgments.

Tips for Success

- To spot facts, ask yourself if a statement could be checked or proven.
- To spot opinions, look for words that show values, such as *worst* or *best*.

As you read this paragraph, think about the facts and opinions the writer uses.

On an average day, 1,000 American children are treated in hospitals for bicycle-related accidents. The most serious are head injuries. About 90 percent of these head wounds could have been avoided with bicycle helmets. Why don't more bicyclists wear helmets? It's ridiculous to claim that helmets are uncomfortable. Yet even if helmets were a bother, it's a small price to pay to avoid a serious injury. I think people simply haven't gotten into the habit of wearing helmets yet. Our state must begin a major campaign to boost helmet use. We owe it to ourselves.

1. Which statement is a fact?

   A. Our state must begin a major campaign to boost helmet use.

   B. Even if helmets were a bother, it's a small price to pay to avoid a serious injury.

   C. It's ridiculous to claim that helmets are uncomfortable.

   D. About 90 percent of these head wounds could have been avoided with bicycle helmets.

1. Ⓐ Ⓑ Ⓒ Ⓓ **Mark your answer choice by filling in the oval.**

 Now check to see whether you chose the correct answer.

   A. The word *must* indicates that this is an opinion. There's no way to prove that this campaign must occur.

   B. While most people would agree with this statement, it's still an opinion. The writer feels or believes it's a small price.

   C. The word *ridiculous* shows a judgment. There's no way to prove this claim is ridiculous.

   D. This is the correct answer. You could check with medical authorities to find out whether this statement is a fact.

As you read this letter, look for facts and opinions.

To the Editor:

Do you know where your dog is right now? I ask because too many people are ignoring New Hope's leash laws. I wouldn't have thought it was a problem until last Sunday when three unfamiliar dogs ran into my yard and attacked my cat Ali. She was wounded badly and died in the car on the way to the vet. According to the vet, Ali was the fourth cat in town to die this way! These deaths are an unnecessary tragedy.

The dogs that are running loose are not bad dogs. It's an instinct for dogs to run in packs. The dog owners, however, are being irresponsible. They are the **culpable** ones! Over 30 loose dogs were hit by cars last year in New Hope. Also, the number of rabies cases among raccoons is now at an all-time high in the state. Loose dogs could attack these animals and get sick.

The law says dogs in New Hope must be on a leash at all times. If your neighbors ignore this law, please speak to them. I don't want to cause problems among people in town. However, the death of poor Ali forces me to speak out.

Emi Park

---

1. Ⓐ Ⓑ Ⓒ Ⓓ
2. Ⓐ Ⓑ Ⓒ Ⓓ
3. Ⓐ Ⓑ Ⓒ Ⓓ

Mark the best answer for questions 1–3.

1. Which statement is a fact?

   A. The dogs that are running loose are not bad dogs.

   B. The number of rabies cases among raccoons is now at an all-time high in the state.

   C. Too many people are ignoring New Hope's leash laws.

   D. These deaths of pet cats are an unnecessary tragedy.

2. Which statement is an opinion?

   A. Over 30 loose dogs were hit by cars last year in New Hope.

   B. The dog owners, however, are being irresponsible.

   C. It's an instinct for dogs to run in packs.

   D. Ali was the fourth cat in town to die this way!

3. You can figure out that **culpable** in paragraph 2 means

   A. understanding.

   B. unconcerned.

   C. guilty.

   D. freedom-loving.

4. Choose one of the facts in the letter. Tell how you might check or prove it.

_____

_____

_____

_____

Comparison and Contrast

To **compare** is to look at ways in which two things are similar. To **contrast** is to focus on the ways in which two things are different. Persuasive text often uses comparison and contrast to develop a main idea.

Suppose, for example, a newspaper editorial wants readers to vote for a new candidate for state government. The editorial might first tell how the present governor failed to solve problems with the environment, unemployment, and crime. Then, point by point, the editorial might tell how the new candidate plans to deal with these same problems. This comparison and contrast might persuade many readers to vote for the new candidate.

Tips for Success

- Decide what is being compared or contrasted.
- Determine which points of comparison support the writer's main idea.

As you read this passage, think about whether the writer compares and contrasts soccer and baseball persuasively.

If you have to decide on a sport to play, consider soccer over baseball. I know most Americans prefer baseball, and you're likely to play for a larger crowd if you play baseball. For other reasons, however, soccer gets my vote. Soccer provides better exercise since you're running after the ball the whole time. I must run 5 miles in a game. In baseball, I stand around half the time waiting for the ball to be hit to me. The rest of the time, I sit on a bench waiting to hit. Soccer also requires less equipment. One ball and a grassy field are all a team needs. Baseball players need bats, gloves, balls, a backstop, a pitcher's mound, and baselines. I also prefer soccer because it's safer. Fast balls, swinging bats, and sliding runners cause serious injuries in baseball. In soccer, players run into each other, but on the whole the sport is less dangerous.

1. The writer believes that, compared with baseball, soccer is the better sport because
   A. players get more exercise.
   B. players need more equipment.
   C. soccer is dangerous.
   D. soccer is more popular.

1. Ⓐ Ⓑ Ⓒ Ⓓ

Mark your answer choice by filling in the oval.

✔ **Now check to see whether you chose the correct answer.**

A. This is the correct answer. The writer states that in baseball, players stand around more.

B. According to the passage, players need less equipment in soccer.

C. The author claims safety is a point in favor of soccer.

D. The author says Americans prefer baseball over soccer and are more likely to attend baseball games.

Read this persuasive article about a new medical invention.

Medical Glue or Stitches?

Have you ever gotten such a bad cut that you needed to get stitches? At least 11 million Americans have wounds stitched up in hospital emergency rooms every year. Can you imagine having those bad cuts simply glued shut with special medical glue? The idea of medical glue seems weird to us because it isn't used in the United States. Doctors here still rely on stitches to close wounds. In Canada, Israel, and Japan, however, more and more doctors are using a special medical glue instead of stitches. I think it's time that Americans start to benefit from this important new advance, too.

Medical glue is nontoxic and works on most cuts. Moreover, the new glue is relatively painless. Closing a wound with glue is also fast, taking only one-quarter the time of stitching.

Furthermore, no expensive follow-up visit is necessary to remove the stitches. Faster, less painful, less expensive—don't you agree that this is an invention whose time has come?

The authorities continue to weigh the pros and cons of the new glue even though the facts are already in. Wounds treated with glue heal in about the same time as stitches. What's more, specialists see no difference in the appearance of the scar, if any, after healing. That's not to say the glue doesn't have drawbacks. Deep wounds still require stitching. The glue can't be used on the hands or on parts of the body that bend a lot since the constant movement causes the glue to peel or flake off. For most wounds, however, the glue works great, and I say it's time we put it to work in the United States.

---

1. Ⓐ Ⓑ Ⓒ Ⓓ
2. Ⓐ Ⓑ Ⓒ Ⓓ

Mark the best answer for questions 1–2.

1. The writer notes several contrasts between stitching and gluing. One contrast that might persuade the reader to favor the glue is
   A. the treatment of hand wounds.
   B. the scar left by a wound.
   C. the time it takes for a wound to heal.
   D. the pain involved in treating a wound.

2. Why does the writer compare America to Canada, Japan, and Israel?
   A. Canada, Japan, and Israel are devleoping countries.
   B. Canada, Japan, and Israel favor stitches over glue.
   C. Medical glue is used in those countries safely.
   D. More of the citizens in those countries are doctors.

3. Why might you ask your doctor to use medical glue to close a wound?

_____

_____

_____

Persuasive Text

45

In these pages, you can use the skills you have practiced in this chapter. Read the editorials and answer the questions. Mark your answer choices by filling in the ovals.

The Case Against Video Games
by Lydia Montez

1. I realize that video games are wildly popular and are probably here to stay. Nevertheless I think it's important to explain why they should not be available in the computer lab here in King School.

2. One reason that I am against video games is their violence. I realize not all games are violent. However, the best-selling games deal with martial arts, war, and other violent themes. Taking part in all that shooting, punching, and kicking has to make a person more aggressive. A former surgeon general of the United States cited this problem, concluding that there was "nothing constructive" about video games. Why introduce destructive material into our school?

3. Another problem with video games is that they are a waste of time. In order to get a high score or win, you have to play for hours and hours. According to one study, 40 percent of boys with computers spend two hours a day on the games. We're only in school six and a half hours a day. That time should be put to better use than playing games.

4. I've also noticed that the kids who are glued to video games have little time for real-life activities. For example, my cousins play video football and basketball all the time. However, they never play these sports outside on the field. So they miss the real benefits of sports, such as improving physical fitness and being part of a team. Instead, they are out of shape and isolated, staring mindlessly at a screen.

5. Supporters claim these games develop eye-hand coordination. That may be true. However, almost any activity—baseball, sewing, painting— would develop coordination, too.

6. I suspect that video game players develop "fast forward" minds. They are so used to the fast pace and high action of their games that they find it hard to slow down for activities that require more thought. One in four kids is already labeled hyperactive in this school. Video games in the classroom will make the problem worse.

7. Finally, I have to say that the video game characters and plots are boring. In good books and movies, characters have different sides and traits. The plots are intriguing. Game characters, however, are one-dimensional. Stereotypes, such as macho he-men and helpless females, are typical. Similarly, the game plots are all **hackneyed** and totally predictable. They just depend on fast action and colorful graphics to grab a player's interest. For these and other reasons, I think making video games available during school hours is a big mistake.

The Case for Video Games
by Major Greye

1. I think video games have a positive role to play in our lives. Like TV, video games are primarily entertainment. TV viewers, however, watch the screen passively, while video game players are actively involved with what's on the screen. Studies show that game players are in a more relaxed state of mind than TV viewers. Also, many games let you play against a friend. In other games, two players can play against the computer or game machine. So video games promote human interaction and cooperation.

2. Video games are also educational. Some games teach specific skills—such as math or geography—in a fun way. So if you're weak in a certain subject, a video game might be a way to improve. Other games develop skills in less obvious ways. For example, winning a video game often requires you to focus closely on something and react quickly. Those games develop a player's concentration and eye-hand coordination. That coordination will help in countless real-life activities, such as sports, art, driving, and crafts.

3. Playing video games also builds self-confidence. Not everyone can excel in academics or sports. Video games present a real challenge and give many students an arena in which to succeed. Winning a game is a real achievement. The games even record high scores and the names of the top players. Video games can be programmed for different levels of difficulty. So they encourage players to get better and better. Players learn an important lesson: Determination and effort pay off in the end. Many games also require a player to figure out a winning strategy and stick with it. This is another important skill that video game players can apply to real life to heighten their chances for success.

4. Playing video games also helps young people learn about computers. I play on a computer, and as a result, I have become fairly computer literate. I know how to load programs, and I can check the files on my hard drive. I also installed more memory in my computer last summer.

5. I know many people complain about video games. The main objection seems to be that it's unhealthy for kids to spend so much time playing them. I can understand that. But the solution to that seems easy: Set time limits on how long you will play. Then you can enjoy video games without letting them interfere with the rest of your life.

6. Finally, I'd like to say that computer games are here to stay. Kids are going to play them at home and at the arcades, and the games can be a positive force in education. I think the school should find games that are interesting, exciting, and educational for use in the computer room. They can be used to teach or as a reward for students who have completed their work.

1. Ⓐ Ⓑ Ⓒ Ⓓ
2. Ⓐ Ⓑ Ⓒ Ⓓ
3. Ⓐ Ⓑ Ⓒ Ⓓ
4. Ⓐ Ⓑ Ⓒ Ⓓ
5. Ⓐ Ⓑ Ⓒ Ⓓ
6. Ⓐ Ⓑ Ⓒ Ⓓ

MAIN IDEA

1. What is the main idea of Lydia's editorial?

   A. Video games are too violent.

   B. Video games shouldn't be available in school.

   C. Video games are predictable and boring.

   D. Video games waste time that could be better spent.

SUPPORTING DETAILS

2. Which detail in Lydia's editorial BEST supports her main idea?

   A. A former surgeon general concluded that there was "nothing constructive" about video games.

   B. Playing video games develops eye-hand coordination.

   C. Video games are wildly popular and here to stay.

   D. Video game characters are one-dimensional.

FACT AND OPINION

3. Which statement from Lydia's editorial is a fact?

   A. Most video games are really boring.

   B. Taking part in all that shooting and punching and kicking has to make a person more aggressive.

   C. One in four kids is already labeled hyperactive in this school.

   D. I suspect that video game players develop "fast forward" minds.

COMPARISON AND CONTRAST

4. Lydia compares video games to baseball, sewing, and painting to show that

   A. kids' activities don't have to be boring.

   B. many activities develop coordination.

   C. many activities provide kids with a sense of accomplishment.

   D. constructive activities can be done alone or with others.

VOCABULARY

5. The context of Lydia's last paragraph suggests that the word **hackneyed** means

   A. colorful.

   B. hyperactive.

   C. worn-out.

   D. computer-related.

MAIN IDEA

6. What is the main idea of Major's editorial?

   A. Video games are here to stay.

   B. Video games are educational.

   C. Students learn more from video games than from traditional methods of education.

   D. Video games can play a positive role in students' lives.

FACT AND OPINION

7. Which statement from Major's editorial is a fact?

A. Video games encourage players to get better and better.

B. Playing video games also builds self-confidence.

C. Studies show that game players are in a more relaxed state of mind than TV viewers.

D. If you're weak in a certain subject, a video game might help you improve.

SUPPORTING DETAILS

8. Which detail does Major NOT offer in his editorial?

A. Millions of successful professional people enjoy video games regularly.

B. Video games help young people become computer literate.

C. Video games are interactive and so are healthier than TV viewing.

D. Winning at video games gives people a sense of achievement.

COMPARISON AND CONTRAST

9. Both Lydia and Major seem to agree that

A. frequent players of video games have "fast forward" minds.

B. video games build self-confidence.

C. the games improve eye-hand coordination.

D. video games depend on colorful graphics and fast action to grab a player's interest.

FACT AND OPINION

10. Which statement BEST describes the content of the editorials?

A. Lydia uses mainly facts while Major relies on opinions.

B. Major uses mainly facts while Lydia relies on opinions.

C. Both writers use a mix of both facts and opinions.

D. Both writers rely mainly on opinions.

7.	Ⓐ	Ⓑ	Ⓒ	Ⓓ
8.	Ⓐ	Ⓑ	Ⓒ	Ⓓ
9.	Ⓐ	Ⓑ	Ⓒ	Ⓓ
10.	Ⓐ	Ⓑ	Ⓒ	Ⓓ

11. Who do you think made a stronger argument, Lydia or Major? State your opinion and summarize two points that he or she made that you thought were most persuasive.

_____

_____

_____

_____

The final type of text that will appear on the reading test is **everyday text**. Here are some questions you might have about this type of text.

 What is everyday text?
Everyday text is reading material that you might use at home, in school, or in the community. Usually, it contains information that you need to know in order to accomplish something practical.

 What types of reading materials are everyday texts?
Everyday texts are a common part of your life. They include movie schedules, recipes, rules and regulations, directions for making something, food labels, flyers, mail-order catalogs, and computer manuals.

 What are the major elements of everyday text?
Because everyday texts are so varied, they have different elements.

- The **relevant data** in an everyday text is the information you need to achieve a specific purpose.

- A **sequence of data** shows you the order of steps you need to do or make something.

- Often, you need to organize or **classify** information in everyday text in order to make a choice or reach a logical conclusion.

- Sometimes you need to **synthesize** or combine the information from one or more everyday texts to make real-life decisions or judgments.

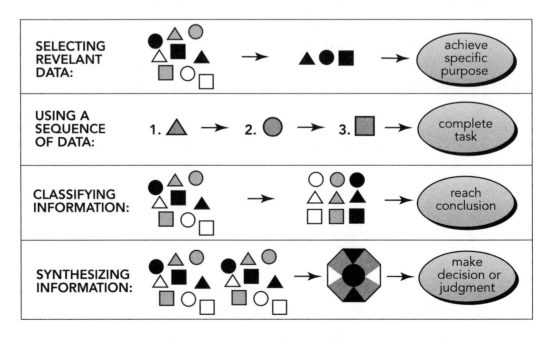

Test Questions About Everyday Text

The following questions about everyday text come from actual tests. Studying them will help you become familiar with the most common types of test questions about everyday text.

Questions About Selecting Relevant Data

- What percentage of the daily requirement for vitamin C is contained in an 8-ounce glass of Perk-Up?
- When does the 1:00 P.M. bus from Preston arrive in Center City?
- At which field will the girls' softball team practice on Thursdays?
- When does the last showing of *Killer Creature* begin?
- What is the book club price for a paperback copy of *Division Two*?

Questions About Using a Sequence of Data

- What is the last step in making the mobile?
- Immediately before entering the water from a boat, a scuba diver must _____.
- After adding the egg-white-and-cream mixture, the cook next _____.
- At what intervals should you give the medicine to a four-year-old with a high fever?

Questions About Classifying Information

- Which book would Robert probably NOT like?
- The BEST class for Em to take on Saturday would be _____.
- Which job pays the least?
- Kim must be home by 10 P.M. If it takes her 20 minutes to walk home from the theater, which movie will she be UNABLE to go to?

Questions About Synthesizing Information

- Which of the summer jobs would work out BEST for Dan?
- How would you rate Jen's chances for making the swim team?
- Based on what you know about the members of the Martinez family, which vacation seems to fit their needs BEST?
- Why was buying a Speedwell mountain bike NOT a good decision for Bonnie?

The lessons in Chapter 4 will help you understand how to answer test questions about everyday texts. You'll read some short everyday texts and answer a few questions about each. The upcoming lessons will also help you synthesize the information in everyday texts in a way that will make it easier for you to make decisions and draw conclusions.

Selecting Relevant Data

You encounter everyday text all the time. You read the label on a cereal box over breakfast. You check a schedule or calendar on the way to school. You follow signs and directions to get to class.

You will often check everyday text when you need to make a decision. The text contains the **relevant data**, or information you need. You have to find the relevant or necessary information and decide how to use it.

Tips for Success

• Look for specific pieces of information in the text that will answer the question.

• Combine different pieces of information in a text to choose the correct answer.

Study this food label. It shows the nutrition facts in a box of vegetable burger mix.

NATURE'S BEST ALL-VEGETABLE BURGER MIX

Nutrition Facts
Serving Size 1/4 cup (47 g)
Servings Per Container 6

Amount Per Serving	% Daily Value*
Calories 170	
Calories from Fat 25	
Total Fat 3 g	5%
Saturated Fat 0 g	0%
Cholesterol 0 mg	0%
Sodium 320 mg	13%
Total Carbohydrates 30 g	10%
Dietary Fiber 5 g	20%
Sugars 2 g	
Protein 8 g	

*Percent Daily Values are based on a 2,000 calorie diet. Your daily values may be higher or lower depending on your calorie needs.

Vitamin A   4% • Vitamin C   4% • Calcium   6% • Iron   10%

1. Raoul and Nilda cook for their grandfather on weekends. He is on a low-fat, low-sodium diet. If they serve him two vegetable burgers, he would get approximately

A. 3 g of fat.

B. 26 mg of sodium.

C. 10 g of fat.

D. 640 mg of sodium.

1. Ⓐ Ⓑ Ⓒ Ⓓ

Mark your answer choice by filling in the oval.

Now check to see whether you chose the correct answer.

A. One vegetable burger has 3 g of fat.

B. Two burgers would have 640 mg of sodium, not 26 mg.

C. Two burgers would have 6 g of fat, not 10 g.

D. This is the correct answer. At 320 mg of sodium each, two burgers would contain 640 mg.

Read this schedule. Then answer the questions that follow.

Madison County Summer Recreation Schedule

Dates	Subject	Time	Location
SESSION I			
June 10, 17, 24	Square Dancing	7:00–8:45 P.M.	Center Park
June 12, 19, 26	Photography	6:00–7:30 P.M.	Lafayette School
June 14, 21, 28	Poetry Workshop	7:00–9:15 P.M.	Oakhill Library
June 12, 16, 23	Oil Painting	3:30–5:00 P.M.	Royal Hall
SESSION 2			
July 1, 8, 15	Ceramics	3:00–5:00 P.M.	Brewer Street Studio
July 3, 10, 17	Drama Workshop	4:00–6:00 P.M.	Lafayette School
July 7, 14, 21	Kite-Flying	9:30–11:30 A.M.	Weatherill Arboretum
July 3, 7, 10	Handmade Instruments	1:00–4:00 P.M.	Oakhill Library
SESSION 3			
August 2, 5, 10	Sculpture	2:00–5:00 P.M.	Brewer Street Studio
August 3, 6, 9	Landscape Painting	9:00–11:30 A.M.	Center Park
August 4, 7, 10	Fun with Paper	10:00 A.M.–noon	Eden Hill *Park*
August 5, 9, 14	Stand-up Comics	1:00–4:00 P.M.	Royal Hall

1. Ⓐ Ⓑ Ⓒ Ⓓ
2. Ⓐ Ⓑ Ⓒ Ⓓ
3. Ⓐ Ⓑ Ⓒ Ⓓ
4. Ⓐ Ⓑ Ⓒ Ⓓ

Mark the best answer for questions 1–4.

1. Ruth will be out of town until the end of June. Then she'll be home for just 12 days before going to camp for the rest of the summer. What activity can she take if she wants to attend all three classes?

   A. Ceramics

   B. Drama Workshop

   C. Kite-Flying

   D. Handmade Instruments

2. Toni wants to take a class during Session I. Because her mother works evenings, she'll have to walk to class. Only Center Park is within walking distance. What class can Toni take?

   A. Square Dancing

   B. Photography

   C. Poetry Workshop

   D. Oil Painting

3. Jack plans to take the Session 3 class that meets at Royal Hall. What days will he need to be there?

   A. August 2, 5, 10

   B. August 3, 6, 9

   C. August 4, 7, 10

   D. August 5, 9, 14

4. Min wants to take a class, but she works from 3:00–7:30 P.M. every day, and she is going away on vacation for the whole month of August. What class can she take?

   A. Poetry Workshop

   B. Landscape Painting

   C. Sculpture

   D. Kite-Flying

Lesson 2 Using a Sequence of Data

Whether you like to cook, play games, build things, work with computers, or sew, you're bound to come across everyday reading that tells you how to make or do something. Being able to follow directions will allow you to do many things. When reading directions, go through them quickly at first to get a general idea of what you have to do. Then read them again more carefully.

Since directions are an important part of everyday reading, you usually find them on reading tests. Often you have to identify which step comes *first*, *second*, or *last*. You may also have to tell which step comes *before* or *after* another step.

Tips for Success

- Look in the text for the specific words and phrases used in a question. The answer will often be nearby.
- Look for words that show time and order: *first, second, next, last, then, finally.*

As you read these directions, think about each step.

Here's a quick way to grow bean sprouts. Put about 2 tablespoons of bean seeds into a wide-mouthed jar and cover with at least three-quarters of a cup of warm water. Let the seeds soak overnight. In the morning, pour the water off the swollen seeds. Then rinse with warm water. Drain well and return to the jar. Cover the opening of the jar with two layers of cheesecloth held in place with a rubber band. Keep the jar in a dark place. Rinse the seeds with warm water morning and night. The spouts should be about 1 inch long in two or three days. When they're 2 to 3 inches long, place the jar in the refrigerator to stop the growth. You can eat the entire sprout—root, seed, and even the tiny leaves if there are any.

1. About how much time will pass before you put the bean sprouts in the refrigerator?

    A. one day

    B. two days

    C. three days

    D. more than three days

1. Ⓐ Ⓑ Ⓒ Ⓓ

Mark your answer choice by filling in the oval.

Now check to see whether you chose the correct answer.

    A. After just one day, the seeds will have barely sprouted.

    B. Reread the directions. More than two days have to pass.

    C. The sprouts will be one inch long in two to three days, but they have to be two to three inches before you stop their growth.

    D. This is the correct answer. It will take more than two or three days for the sprouts to be long enough to stop their growth.

Read these directions. Then answer the questions that follow.

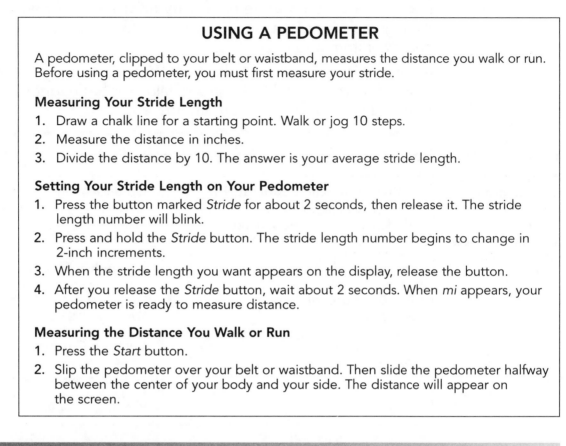

USING A PEDOMETER

A pedometer, clipped to your belt or waistband, measures the distance you walk or run. Before using a pedometer, you must first measure your stride.

Measuring Your Stride Length
1. Draw a chalk line for a starting point. Walk or jog 10 steps.
2. Measure the distance in inches.
3. Divide the distance by 10. The answer is your average stride length.

Setting Your Stride Length on Your Pedometer
1. Press the button marked *Stride* for about 2 seconds, then release it. The stride length number will blink.
2. Press and hold the *Stride* button. The stride length number begins to change in 2-inch increments.
3. When the stride length you want appears on the display, release the button.
4. After you release the *Stride* button, wait about 2 seconds. When *mi* appears, your pedometer is ready to measure distance.

Measuring the Distance You Walk or Run
1. Press the *Start* button.
2. Slip the pedometer over your belt or waistband. Then slide the pedometer halfway between the center of your body and your side. The distance will appear on the screen.

1. Ⓐ Ⓑ Ⓒ Ⓓ
2. Ⓐ Ⓑ Ⓒ Ⓓ
3. Ⓐ Ⓑ Ⓒ Ⓓ

Mark the best answer for questions 1–3.

1. What is the first thing to do when using the pedometer for the first time?
    A. Press the *Start* button.
    B. Slip the pedometer over your belt or waistband.
    C. Measure your stride length.
    D. Release the *Stride* button.

2. You will know your pedometer is ready to measure distance when
    A. you hear two short beeps.
    B. *mi* appears on the screen.
    C. two zeros blink on the screen.
    D. the stride length number is blinking.

3. To measure your stride length, you must
    A. estimate the distance from a chalk line to the start of your route.
    B. measure the distance you walk in 2 seconds.
    C. press the button marked stride for 2 seconds and then release it.
    D. measure the distance of 10 steps and divide by 10.

Lesson 3 Classifying Information

In order to complete tasks or make decisions, people often need information. You organize or **classify information** when you look through an everyday text, discard the information you don't need, and find the information you do need.

A catalog is a typical everyday text. What sorts of information would you look for as you leafed through a catalog? What might you think about before deciding to order something?

Tips for Success

- Keep in mind the decision that has to be made.
- Go through all the possibilities. Check off any that don't work.

Read this page from a book-and-craft catalog.

Native American Beadcraft Kit

Learn how to make beaded belts, headbands, necklaces, and more! Kit includes traditional loom, materials, and instructions.
You pay **$9.95**

The Big Book of Puzzles and Mazes

Test your wits against the greatest puzzle masters of the world.
You pay **$7.95**

Up and Away Kite Kit

Fly a kite you've made yourself. Includes materials and easy-to-follow instructions.
You pay **$4.95**

A Laugh a Minute

3,600 jokes to keep your funny bone rattling all day.
You pay **$3.50**

Cartoon Cut-ups

50 of your favorite animal cartoon figures on postcards you can cut out to trade or send.
You pay **$4.95**

---

1. Genelle wants to order a birthday present from the catalog for her cousin. She has $5 to spend. Her cousin loves to spend time outdoors and also likes making things. What would probably be the BEST gift?

A. *Native American Beadcraft Kit*

B. *A Laugh a Minute*

C. *Up and Away Kite Kit*

D. *Cartoon Cut-ups*

1. Ⓐ Ⓑ Ⓒ Ⓓ **Mark your answer choice by filling in the oval.**

✓ **Now check to see whether you chose the correct answer.**

A. This would be a good gift, but it costs more than Genelle wants to spend.

B. Genelle could afford this book, but would her cousin like it?

C. This is the correct answer. The price is right and a kite is something to make and use outdoors.

D. Genelle could afford this, but the kite kit is probably the better gift.

Test Practice   Use this moviegoer's guide to answer the questions below.

WELCOME TO THE QUADRIPLEX CINEMA!
Adults: $7 Children under 13: $4.50
Matinees: All Seats $3 Last Matinee 3:00 P.M.

The Beast Among Us
2:30, 4:40, 7:45, 10:00
Pleasanton is a typical All-American small town. Too bad one of the neighbors is a beast! Will the good folks find the monster before it's too late?
Starring Brad Flynn and Gwen Free.

Wait Until Spring
3:00, 4:50, 6:50, 9:00
With its avalanches, polar bears, -50°F weather, being stranded in backcountry Alaska would test the mettle of the toughest mountain man. Benny White is a city kid from Chicago's South Side. How's he going to survive?
Starring Chad Shaw and Dana Blue.

Night Cover
3:30, 6:00, 8:20, 10:40
Operating behind enemy lines, a crack American commando team attempts to disrupt German supply lines. Does the fate of its men rest in the hands of a turncoat spy?
Starring Max Lagerfelt and Mimi Weiss.

Triple Trouble
1:00, 4:00, 7:50, 9:50
Not only are Rex, Rod, and Rory identical triplets, they're also dyed-in-the-wool tricksters! Upscale Preston Heights will never be the same once this troublesome trio moves to town!
Starring Benny Gomez and Wilson Flute.

---

1. Ⓐ Ⓑ Ⓒ Ⓓ
2. Ⓐ Ⓑ Ⓒ Ⓓ
3. Ⓐ Ⓑ Ⓒ Ⓓ

Mark the best answer for questions 1–3.

1. Jan and Denise arrive at the Quadriplex at 7:30 P.M. Jan doesn't like scary movies, and the girls have to be out by 10:00 P.M. to get their ride home. What movie might be BEST for Jan and Denise?
   A. *The Beast Among Us*
   B. *Wait Until Spring*
   C. *Night Cover*
   D. *Triple Trouble*

2. While shopping at the mall, Mr. Chen promised to take his two young daughters to a movie. It's 2:45 P.M. and Mr. Chen would like to take advantage of matinee prices if possible. What movie might be the BEST choice for the Chens?
   A. *The Beast Among Us*
   B. *Wait Until Spring*
   C. *Night Cover*
   D. *Triple Trouble*

3. Teddy is 14 and Ernie is 12. When their soccer game ends at 2:00 P.M., they head straight to the mall. How much will it cost for both of them to see *Night Cover*?
   A. $6
   B. $9
   C. $11.50
   D. $14

Synthesizing Information

Synthesizing is putting different things together to make a whole. Sometimes you will draw different parts of the information you need from different sources. Then, by putting it together, you will have the information you need to make a decision or judgment.

Tips for Success

• Study the text carefully.

• Keep in mind what you're trying to decide.

• Go through all the possibilities.

The National Fresh Water Fishing Hall of Fame keeps records of the biggest fish ever caught in the United States. Use the following records to answer the question below.

THE BIGGEST SPORT FISH EVER CAUGHT

Largemouth Bass
22 pounds 4 ounces
1932

Blue Catfish
109 pounds 4 ounces
1991

King Salmon
97 pounds 4 ounces
1985

Smallmouth Bass
11 pounds 15 ounces
1955

Muskellunge
69 pounds 11 ounces
1949

Rainbow Trout
42 pounds 2 ounces
1970

Bluegill
4 pounds 12 ounces
1950

Yellow Perch
4 pounds 3 ounces
1865

Lake Trout
66 pounds 8 ounces
1987

Carp
57 pounds 13 ounces
1983

Northern Pike
46 pounds 2 ounces
1940

---

1. Which of the following catches reported to the Fishing Hall of Fame might qualify as a new record?

   A. a 63-pound, 4-ounce muskellunge

   B. a 41-pound, 11-ounce rainbow trout

   C. a 12-pound, 1-ounce smallmouth bass

   D. an 83-pound, 7-ounce blue catfish

1. Ⓐ Ⓑ Ⓒ Ⓓ   **Mark your answer choice by filling in the oval.**

✔ **Now check to see whether you chose the correct answer.**

   A. There have been bigger muskellunge caught than this.

   B. This trout isn't bigger than the one caught in 1970.

   C. This is the correct answer. The previous record fish weighed just under 12 pounds.

   D. The record blue catfish was more than 20 pounds heavier than this.

Test Practice   A local shop on Green Lake hands out this flyer to vacationers.

WHEN TO FISH IN GREEN LAKE

Early Season Fishing (March, April, May)

Early Morning (6:00–9:00 A.M.)   Fishing: *Slow*
Cool water temperature and low angle of sun's rays.

Late Morning/Early Afternoon (9:00 A.M.–1:00 P.M.)   Fishing: *Irregular*
Sun starts to penetrate water and surface warms up.

Late Afternoon/Evening (1:00–5:00 P.M.)   Fishing: *Best*
Sun's rays penetrate water to maximum depth.

Mid-Season Fishing (mid-June—mid-September)

Early Morning (4:30–9:00 A.M.)   Fishing: *Best*
Fish active before daybreak to till water heats up.

Mid-Morning/Late Afternoon (9:00 A.M.–7:00 P.M.)   Fishing: *Poor*
Fish are inactive and in deepest water.

Sunset/Evening (7:00–9:00 P.M.)   Fishing: *Best*
Fish become active again after sunset.

Late-Season Fishing (mid-September—ice-up)

Early Morning (Daybreak–9:00 A.M.)   Fishing: *Poor*
Cool water temperatures and little sun penetration leave fish inactive.

Late Morning (9:00 A.M.–Noon)   Fishing: *Irregular*
Fish are active in shallow water.

Afternoon/Evening (Noon–6 P.M.)   Fishing: *Best*
Fish are most active in warmer surface water.

---

1. Ⓐ Ⓑ Ⓒ Ⓓ
2. Ⓐ Ⓑ Ⓒ Ⓓ
3. Ⓐ Ⓑ Ⓒ Ⓓ
4. Ⓐ Ⓑ Ⓒ Ⓓ

Mark the best answer for questions 1–4.

1. In early spring, the best time to fish in Green Lake is
   A. daybreak.
   B. 9 A.M.
   C. noon.
   D. 5:00 P.M.

2. In early fall, you would have the best luck fishing
   A. in the shallow water.
   B. in shady areas.
   C. in surface water.
   D. in the deepest water.

3. Getting up and going fishing at sun-up makes sense in
   A. April.
   B. March.
   C. August.
   D. October.

4. How would the fishing be between 3:00–4:30 P.M. in July?
   A. irregular
   B. poor
   C. best
   D. slow

45 Use these samples of everyday text to practice the skills you've learned in this chapter. Read the texts and answer the questions. Mark your answer choices by filling in the ovals.

Use this bus schedule to answer questions 1–4.

WEEKDAY MORNING BUS SERVICE: AVERY TO STATEVILLE					
State & Lincoln	Curry & Harlan	Route 11 Alton	Big 6 Mall	Pine Plaza	City Hall
6:10	6:28	—	6:40	6:48	7:20
6:25	—	—	7:13	7:25	8:05
6:50	7:08	7:15	7:20	7:28	7:58
—	—	—	7:43	7:55	8:22
7:40	7:58	—	8:10	8:18	8:45
—	—	8:10	8:15	8:25	8:48

1. Ⓐ Ⓑ Ⓒ Ⓓ
2. Ⓐ Ⓑ Ⓒ Ⓓ
3. Ⓐ Ⓑ Ⓒ Ⓓ
4. Ⓐ Ⓑ Ⓒ Ⓓ

SELECT RELEVANT DATA

1. If Carlo boards the bus at Curry and Harlan streets at 7:58, when should he arrive at City Hall?

   A. 8:18
   B. 8:22
   C. 8:45
   D. 8:48

SELECT RELEVANT DATA

2. Connie just missed the 7:20 bus at the Big 6 Mall. When will the next bus arrive?

   A. 7:28
   B. 7:43
   C. 7:55
   D. 8:10

SELECT RELEVANT DATA

3. Ari must reach Pine Plaza by 8:30. What is the latest time he can take a bus from State and Lincoln streets?

   A. 6:10
   B. 6:25
   C. 6:50
   D. 7:40

SELECT RELEVANT DATA

4. Vin boards the bus at Route 11 Alton at 7:15. How long does it take him to arrive at City Hall?

   A. 38 minutes
   B. 50 minutes
   C. 13 minutes
   D. 43 minutes

Use these directions to answer questions 5–8.

5. Ⓐ Ⓑ Ⓒ Ⓓ
6. Ⓐ Ⓑ Ⓒ Ⓓ
7. Ⓐ Ⓑ Ⓒ Ⓓ
8. Ⓐ Ⓑ Ⓒ Ⓓ

REPLACING THE TONER CARTRIDGE OF THE LEX 400 PRINTER

1. Turn off the printer and open the lid.
2. Unlock, remove, and discard the used cartridge.
3. Shake the new toner cartridge from side to side to distribute the toner.
4. Hold the cartridge with the red arrow pointing away from you. Slip your fingers under the yellow tabs and pull toward you. The tabs should pop out easily.
5. Peel the tape off the bottom of the cartridge.
6. Position the toner cartridge with the arrow facing the back of the printer.
7. Line up the grooves on the ends of the cartridge with the guides in the image drum assembly.
8. Lower the cartridge into the printer and press down on both ends.
9. Push the two blue locking tabs forward until they catch the lips on the end caps with a click. Continue to push the tabs until they're all the way forward and you hear a second click.

USE SEQUENCE OF DATA

5. Before you peel the tape off the cartridge, you should
   A. shake the new cartridge to distribute the toner.
   B. lower the cartridge into the machine.
   C. push the two blue tabs forward.
   D. hear the first click.

USE SEQUENCE OF DATA

6. You should line up the grooves on the ends of the cartridge with
   A. the blue tabs.
   B. the red arrow.
   C. the guides in the image drum assembly.
   D. the lips on the end caps.

USE SEQUENCE OF DATA

7. How many clicks should you hear before you know that the new toner cartridge is in place in the printer?
   A. one
   B. two
   C. three
   D. none

USE SEQUENCE OF DATA

8. If you want to print out something, what should you do after you have replaced the cartridge?
   A. Push the two blue locking tabs forward.
   B. Turn the printer back on.
   C. Peel the tape off the bottom of the cartridge.
   D. Lower the cartridge into the printer.

Use this page from a weight-lifting manual to answer questions 9–11.

Getting Stronger

Weight training can help you do better in running, cycling, wrestling, and other sports. It can also give you more energy, improve your posture, and make you feel better about yourself. It's also a lot of fun!

Weight lifting can also be dangerous! So never lift alone. Work out with a safety spotter—a friend who helps you in case the weight becomes too heavy for you.

Bench Press   The bench press develops the showy muscles of the chest and arms.

Lie on a bench and grip the barbell at shoulder width. Slowly lower the bar to your chest at the place where your breastbone ends. Pause, then press the bar back to a locked arms position.

Breathe when you have the bar locked out, not while it is in motion. Never bounce the bar off your chest. Do five sets of 10 presses each.

Curls   Curls build big biceps. Hold a dumbbell in each hand while sitting on the edge of a bench. One at a time, curl the dumbbells until they touch your shoulders. Pause, then lower each dumbbell—one at a time—until you extend your arm fully. Repeat slowly and smoothly. Do two sets of 20 repetitions for each arm. If you use a barbell, you will be working both arms at once.

Back Squats   This lift strengthens your hips and legs, helping you run faster and jump higher. Press a barbell over your head and carefully position it on your shoulders behind your neck. Place your feet a bit wider than your shoulders. Keep your back straight and head up.

Slowly lower into a half squat, as if sitting on a chair. Hold your breath as you squat. Pause a second, then slowly stand. Breathe in as you come up. Do five sets of 12 repetitions.

CLASSIFY

9. To strengthen his leg muscles for track, Ramon should do

   A. curls.

   B. back squats.

   C. bench presses.

   D. curls and back squats.

CLASSIFY

10. Which lift can be done with barbells or dumbbells?

   A. curls

   B. back squats

   C. bench presses

   D. all of the above

CLASSIFY

11. When doing a back squat, Ann places her feet wider than her shoulders, leans forward, and lowers into a half squat. She pauses for a second and then breathes in as she slowly stands.
   A trainer would tell Ann to

   A. place her feet closer together.

   B. lower into a full squat.

   C. breathe out as she slowly stands.

   D. straighten her back.

Use this poster to answer questions 12–13.

12. Ⓐ Ⓑ Ⓒ Ⓓ
13. Ⓐ Ⓑ Ⓒ Ⓓ

RUNNING HOT AND COLD

The 5 Ways Your Body Loses Heat

1. **Radiation:** In 40-degree weather, an unprotected head can lose half of the body's total heat production. In 5-degree weather, three-quarters of your body heat can be lost by radiation.
2. **Convection:** Wind and cold drafts will draw off warm air trapped around your body.
3. **Conduction:** Contact with cold objects drains heat from your body.
4. **Evaporation:** Skin loses heat through sweat or when fluids are spilled on flesh.
5. **Respiration:** Inhaling cool air and exhaling warm air drains body heat.

C.O.L.D: The Way to Stay Warm

Cleanliness: To insulate, clothes need to trap air. If dirt gets in the way, the air has less room to collect.

Overheating: Avoid overheating if at all possible. Remove layers before you start to sweat. Sweat dampens clothes and fills air pockets in fabric. Chilling often follows.

Loose Layers: Always wear layers of loose clothing. Loose clothing allows for plenty of air pockets and won't constrict blood flow.

Dryness: Stay dry at all times. Damp and wet clothes cool a body rapidly. Frostbite or hypothermia may follow.

SYNTHESIZE

12. While icefishing, Ann and Kevin place a board on the ice and rest their feet on it. This is a way to limit

    A. radiation.

    B. convection.

    C. conduction.

    D. evaporation.

SYNTHESIZE

13. In cold weather, why is it better to wear three 1-inch layers of clothing than one 3-inch-thick jacket?

    A. When wearing a jacket, more radiation is likely to occur.

    B. Layers are more likely to stay dry next to your skin.

    C. By removing or adding layers, you can fine-tune your body temperatures.

    D. Jackets tend to have less ventilation than layers.

14. An old saying goes, "When your feet feel cold, put on a hat." What information in the poster suggests there is truth in the old saying?

_____

_____

_____

This Practice Test contains four parts. Each part features one of the four different types of text you have studied in this book—narrative, informational, persuasive, and everyday. As you take each part of the test, keep in mind what you have learned about each type of text. The skills you have practiced will help you read the passages effectively, understand the questions, and answer them successfully.

These pages will test your skills with narrative text. Read the story and answer the questions. Mark your answer choices on the answer sheet provided. The clock symbol tells how much time you have to finish the test.

Carried Away

1. I honestly didn't plan to run away. Not that the thought hadn't occurred to me. Twelve thousand years of loyalty to man hasn't gotten me much. Even so, I didn't run away. I was carried away.

2. Why would I run away from Dave? As a "dog's best friend," Dave isn't bad. He fed me, walked me, scratched my ears, and took me to the park every Sunday. That's where we were last week when I got carried away.

3. We had finished our run, and Dave was watching a stickball game while I checked out the bubble gum on the sidewalk. One boy hit a long fly ball, and I was after it. As a retriever, I had no choice. Chasing things is what I do.

4. The ball sailed over the trees onto Third Street, bounced twice, and flew through the open door of a parked RV. Now if I were a guard dog, I would have stopped right there. Guard dogs respect territorial limits. However, my job is to retrieve things, so into the RV I went.

5. The ball rolled under a chair, and I couldn't quite reach it. I was trying to paw it out when the RV door clicked shut, an engine rumbled into action, and I got carried away.

6. I could have whined or barked, especially when Dave came puffing down the block calling, "Buddy!" Thousands of years of **domestication** told me to bark, but I didn't even yelp. Why not? For one thing, I had had it with that name—*Buddy*. I was a purebred and deserved something better. "Golden Commander" would have been nice, but not "Buddy." Besides, after years of dry kibble in a dull backyard, I was ready for a change.

7. How long I slept, I don't know, but I had a rude awakening. "Henry! An *animal!*" The woman's shriek rattled the tags on my collar. Wishing she knew enough to let sleeping dogs lie, I opened one eye and gave my tail a good-natured thump. She bolted out the door as if I were a wolf. Seconds later Henry was at the door with a cell phone. "Get me the dogcatcher. Hurry! It's an emergency." I don't know why my nap was such an emergency, but I wasn't willing to wait for the dogcatcher to find out. So with a growl to **clear** the doorway, I leaped out of the RV and dogtrotted into the night.

8. I was in some sort of campground, and I couldn't believe the scents! I smelled turtle eggs, raccoon legs, garbage cans, barbecues, pizza crusts . . . By 6:00 A.M. my nose was throbbing. Then came my favorite scent of all—bacon and eggs! A man and a boy near a tent were cooking breakfast. With a friendly woof, I bounded in to join the fun. I wasn't expecting trouble since I'm well-groomed, and everyone knows retrievers are great with kids. Imagine my disappointment when the man shouted, "Be careful! A stray!" and the boy started to cry.

9. *A stray!* I wasn't straying. I was on an adventure—that's all. I gave another woof and a wag. That didn't help. Now the man was hurling a stick at me! Was this a game of fetch? It didn't seem likely, but I intercepted the stick and trotted to the campfire. "Into the truck," the man screamed. "This mutt could be rabid."

10. *Rabid! Mutt!* Why, I had more pedigree than his whole family, and no dog is more even-tempered than a retriever. First Henry in the RV and now this guy; I had just about had it with being man's best friend. Right then and there I decided to head out into the countryside. I guess the call of the wild was barking for me.

11. After all, the countryside is where a dog is meant to be. Open meadows, rippling brooks, leafy woods, howling *coyotes*. . . . That's right, a whole pack of howling coyotes was suddenly chasing me. From their snarling, I knew they weren't there to welcome me as a long-lost cousin at the canine family reunion.

12. I hightailed it out of there as if my life depended on it, which it did. It was nip and tuck for awhile. They were nipping, and I was tucking. After five minutes of running, I was so dog-tired I didn't even see the river. I just sailed off the bank and went with the flow. That was all right since retrievers are bred for water. Coyotes aren't. (So don't let anyone tell you good breeding doesn't matter.) I hit the water with an overpaw doggy paddle, and those coyotes were left barking on the bank!

13. Two miles downstream, I dragged myself ashore and padded back toward town. The next time the wild called, I probably wouldn't answer so quickly. I walked all morning, and the dusty country road turned into a paved suburban one. As the traffic got heavier, I knew I was nearing the city.

14. All that traveling had exhausted me. I was sitting on the sidewalk, trying to decide what to do, when my last adventure rolled by. In fact, it rolled over my tail—a baby stroller complete with baby! "My baby! Save my baby!" a woman was screaming. Somehow, the stroller had gotten away from her at the top of the hill; now it was rolling down toward the busy intersection.

15. The stroller may have gotten away from her, but it wouldn't get away from a retriever! I whipped downhill like a greyhound, leaped like a wolfhound, and snagged that stroller just before it got into a dogfight with a cross-town bus!

16. Humans love to make a fuss, and in ten seconds the street was thick with two-leggers petting me. "He saved the baby!" "What a great dog!" "He's a hero!" I had to agree with them.

17. "But whose dog is he?" a police officer barked. He acted as important as

a police dog. He bent down and read my tag in a loud voice: "Buddy." I cringed.

18. "There's a missing dog named Buddy," a little girl piped up. "I just saw a man put up a flyer on the bulletin board at the health food store." So we all walked over to see who I belonged to. Before long I was being led to a house with an all-too-familiar backyard. Truthfully, though, I was glad to be home. I had had my fun, and Dave made a big fuss over me and promised to take me to the park every day! Besides, to tell you the truth, I was ready for a bowl of dry kibble.

---

1. This story takes place over a period of about

  A. two hours.

  B. one day.

  C. two or three days.

  D. a week.

2. Based on how he feels about his name and his breed, you can tell Buddy is quite

  A. proud.

  B. aggressive.

  C. nervous.

  D. selfish.

3. When Buddy is inside the RV and hears his owner Dave running down the street, he doesn't bark because

  A. he's trying to get the ball out from under the chair.

  B. he's afraid of the dogcatcher.

  C. he is ready for a change of pace.

  D. he doesn't want the owners of the RV to know he is there.

4. How does Buddy save the baby at the end of the story?

  A. by alerting the police officer about the danger

  B. by staging a dogfight at the intersection

  C. by finding the missing poster in the heath food store

  D. by catching and stopping the stroller

5. The action of the story

  A. begins at Buddy and Dave's house and ends on a busy street.

  B. begins in a state campground and ends at a health food store.

  C. begins and ends in a city.

  D. begins in an RV and ends in the countryside.

6. Buddy solves the problem he faces with the coyotes by

  A. hiding in the woods.

  B. jumping into a river.

  C. going back to the campsite.

  D. returning to Dave's house.

7. What does the word **domestication** in paragraph 6 mean?

    A. suffering

    B. breeding

    C. understanding

    D. change

8. At the end of the story, Buddy seems to feel

    A. angry that he has been returned to Dave's house.

    B. content because he has had exciting adventures.

    C. afraid because he knows Dave will be angry with him.

    D. terrified, because he narrowly escaped the coyotes.

9. What does the verb **clear** mean in paragraph 7?

    A. to free from guilt or blame

    B. to pass over, under, or by with space to spare

    C. to open or unlock

    D. to make or become clear

10. Which of these proverbs BEST states a theme of the story?

    A. People who live in glass houses shouldn't throw stones.

    B. Don't put all your eggs in one basket.

    C. Many hands make light work.

    D. The grass often seems greener on the other side of the fence.

11. Which message does the author PROBABLY want readers to learn from this story?

    A. Our country is a nation of dog lovers.

    B. Seeking a change of pace in our lifestyle usually causes disaster.

    C. Dogs have deeper feelings than humans often realize.

    D. Dogs have never really been "man's best friend."

12. How does Buddy's breeding as a retriever both cause problems and also help Buddy solve problems in the story?

_____

_____

_____

_____

13. Buddy the dog, the main character in this story, tells the story. How do you think the story would have been different if Buddy's owner or another human told the story?

_____

_____

_____

_____

These pages will test your skills with informational text. Read the passage and the visual aids to answer the questions. Mark your answer choices on the answer sheet provided. The clock symbol tells how much time you have to finish the test.

Protecting Our Water Resources

1. The people who manage our water resources face serious challenges. Many sources of freshwater that people rely on for drinking, recreation, and industry are contaminated. Underground aquifers, layers of rock or soil through which groundwater can move freely, are being pumped faster than they can be naturally refilled. Humans have also dammed and altered the flow of streams and rivers, destroying the habitats of fish and other species.

2. A watershed is a drainage area for a stream, lake, river, or other body of water. The watershed includes the water body itself, its tributaries, and lands that surround and drain into the body of water. A watershed is sometimes called a drainage basin. The watershed for a river can be called a river basin.

3. Activities occurring in watersheds influence the quantity and quality of water flowing into streams, lakes, and rivers. For example, rains falling on lawns that have been treated with fertilizers carry chemicals into the rivers that drain the watershed. In cities and suburbs, where most land is paved, rainwater runs off ten times faster than on unpaved land. Effluents, or liquid wastes, produced by industries and wastewater treatment plants flow into lakes and rivers. These effluents may harm water plants and animals. The destruction of forests and farmland for new construction also affects water quality. Deforested areas erode more easily, and dirt and other matter washes into rivers and streams. Called sediment, it settles to the bottom and clogs the water.

Best Management Practices

4. Regulating the use of land in a watershed protects the water supplies from pollution. To protect watersheds, guidelines called Best Management

Practices, or BMPs, are followed. The BMPs for cities include the use of porous pavements and flood-storage basins. Porous pavement allows rainwater to seep through it. In this way, rain enters the groundwater instead of running off. Flood-storage basins, such as ponds and underground holding tanks, catch runoff. The water stored in these basins can be treated and used.

5. At construction sites, the BMPs call for spreading crushed stone and using straw bales to slow and trap passing water. Cutting grooves along the slope of a construction site roughens the surface. This also slows the flow of water and helps it seep into the ground. As a result, less sediment flows into the main body of water that drains the area.

6. The BMPs for agricultural areas also reduce runoff. **Tillage**, for example, is kept to a minimum. With less plowing, more plants are left to hold the soil in place. Limiting the number of animals that graze in an area also keeps the soil soft and in place. This limits runoff. Soil loss is also prevented by rotating, or switching, the crops grown in a field.

Recharging Aquifers

7. In the United States, much of the water for drinking and agriculture comes from underground aquifers. Problems arise when groundwater is pumped out faster than it is replaced. The Oglala aquifer, for example, stretches from South Dakota to Texas. In some places, its water level is dropping rapidly. That makes pumping the water more difficult and costly. Overuse of an aquifer may also cause the ground to sink. In Florida, sinkholes form when parts of empty aquifers collapse. In coastal areas, seawater can contaminate a near-empty aquifer.

8. Poorly planned development affects the amount of available groundwater. Certain areas are needed to recharge, or refill, the aquifers. When these areas are paved, water that would have entered the ground runs off instead. In Long Island, New York, many people depend on an aquifer for water. The government there had to acquire many acres of open land that was needed to recharge the aquifers. Otherwise the land would have been developed and paved.

Watershed Planning

9. Rivers flow from upstream to downstream. Activities in the upstream part of a watershed affect water quality downstream. That's why wise planning throughout the watershed is essential.

10. Dams are built along rivers to control floods and to store water for irrigation and other important purposes. But dams have unfavorable consequences, too. By disrupting the flow of a river, dams reduce the amount of rich sediment received by farmlands downstream. Dams can interrupt the life cycles of fish, like salmon, which swim upstream to lay their eggs. Dams also interfere with the normal course of the river's water.

11. Another problem affecting rivers is channelization. This is the straightening, widening, smoothing, and deepening of the channel, or path, of a river. Channelization "improves" water flow and prevents flooding. By making the river more uniform, however, this process often lowers the number of plants and animals that the water can support. When the Kissimmee River in Florida was channelized, its length decreased from 103 miles to 56 miles. As a result, the waterbird populations dropped significantly.

14. The author's main purpose for writing this passage is to
    A. explain why Best Management Practices help insure high water quality.
    B. urge people to preserve and protect the environment of lakes and rivers.
    C. tell about the challenges facing managers of water resources.
    D. name the common sources of pollution in a typical watershed.

15. What is the major idea of paragraph 3?
    A. Deforestation causes sediment that clogs rivers and streams.
    B. Many factors affect the quality and quantity of the water in our waterways.
    C. Effluents can cause serious damage to water plants and animals.
    D. Runoff from cities and suburbs is a major source of water pollution.

16. Which detail supports the major idea of paragraph 6?
    A. Once contaminated, an aquifer may take hundreds of years to be restored.
    B. Contour plowing, or plowing across the slope of the land, prevents runoff.
    C. Soil loss can be limited by rotating crops.
    D. The building of suburbs destroys farmland and has a negative effect on water supplies.

17. Sinkholes may appear when
    A. a river or waterway is channelized.
    B. porous pavements are used in cities.
    C. a dam disrupts the natural flow of a river's water.
    D. too much water is pumped from an aquifer.

18. One problem of channelization is that it
    A. prevents aquifers from recharging.
    B. increases runoff.
    C. damages animal habitats.
    D. causes deforestation.

19. The word **tillage** in paragraph 6 means
    A. runoff reduction.
    B. plowing.
    C. agricultural areas.
    D. grazing.

20. A pickle factory pumps a liquid containing vinegar and food coloring into a river. This liquid is an example of
    A. a sediment.
    B. an effluent.
    C. runoff.
    D. channelization.

21. The main purpose of most of the BMPs seems to be
    A. protecting animal habitats.
    B. improving wastewater treatment.
    C. regulating construction practice.
    D. avoiding runoff.

22. At its widest point in New Mexico, the Colorado River Basin is about

A. 50 miles wide.

B. 100 miles wide.

C. 150 miles wide.

D. 200 miles wide.

23. According to the table of contents below, which chapter might have information about chemicals used to purify a city's drinking water?

Chapter 1: The Water Cycle

Chapter 2: Groundwater Resources

Chapter 3: Water Treatment Systems

Chapter 4: Water Conservation

A. Chapter 1

B. Chapter 2

C. Chapter 3

D. Chapter 4

24. Which volume of the encyclopedia might have information about the role of trees in the water cycle?

Hydrology **H:111**

Irrigation **I:366**

Ocean and Climate **O:211**

Plants and the Cycle of Nature **P:454**

Soil and Water **S:343**

A. Volume I

B. Volume O

C. Volume P

D. Volume S

25. Study the index below. If you wanted to find out what kind of sickness people can get from polluted water, which of the following pages would you look on?

Water management
groundwater, 46–47
river flow, 48–50
watershed, 40–44

Water pollution
diseases from, 15–18
and excess nutrients, 21–23
and runoff, 25–28
sewage, 19–21
types of pollutants, 12–14

A. 19–21

B. 12–14

C. 15–18

D. 48–50

26. According to the graphs shown below, lakes and rivers account for how much of the earth's freshwater?

A. less than 1 percent

B. about 3 percent

C. about 20 percent

D. about 53 percent

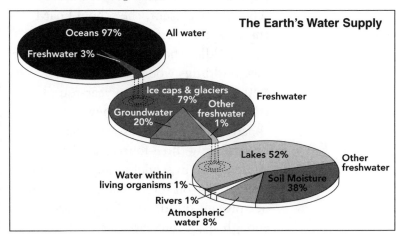

27. Why are environmentalists unlikely to support channelization and dam building? Use details from the passage to support your ideas.

_____

_____

_____

STOP

These pages will test your skills with persuasive text. Read the two editorials and answer the questions that follow. Mark your answer choices on the answer sheet provided. The clock symbol tells how much time you have to finish the test.

Yes to Year-Round Schools
by Martha Hitt

1. The Lincoln School system is proposing a year-round education (YRE) program. Under this program, the schools will be open year-round, including summer. Students will attend school for 60 days and then have 20 days off. The days off are called an intercession. Some people may miss the long summer vacation. Still, the new school calendar will benefit everyone in our school district.

2. As you know, we live in a fast-growing community. As our population increases, we need more schools. At present, the school board thinks a new elementary school and a new middle school must be built. Those new buildings would cost at least $40 million. If we go to year-round education, however, the new construction is unnecessary. That's because only three-fourths of the students are in school at any one time. The rest are on intercession. With YRE, our present buildings will provide enough space for years to come!

3. Saving money isn't the only benefit of YRE. Students also get a better education. Instead of one long 3-month summer break, the kids get three 1-month breaks called intercessions. During intercessions, students can relax, have fun, find jobs, go on vacation, or do volunteer work. Students can also come back to school during intercession to make up absences or to take special classes. Because the schools are always open, they can serve the students better. What's more, under YRE students will be in school 200 days a year. Right now, they only get 175 days of schooling. So YRE is bound to improve student grades and performance.

4. When schools are closed all summer, it's easy to forget what you've learned. A 20-day intercession is less of a problem. So students retain more of what they study. About 45 percent of our students come from homes where English is not the main language. With YRE, they'll be able to master English sooner.

5. The YRE proposal stems from the idea that schools belong to the people. Schools should be open to the people as much as possible. Why should we shut down our centers of learning? Keeping them open means parents and children can use the library and media center all year round. Computers and the Internet will be available, too. The cafeteria can serve nutritious breakfasts and lunches year-round. Those on intercession can come in for meals if they like.

6. Right now, American students

have longer vacations than anyone in the world. "Summer off" education might have worked 100 years ago when most kids lived on farms and had to harvest the crops. Today, we're living in a more challenging time. Schools are too important to close down. It's time for everyone to recognize that!

Year-Round Schools? No Way!
by Sonny Kwon

1. The latest educational **bandwagon** to roll out from the Lincoln School district is year-round schooling. Like most bandwagons, it's loaded with problems. Anyone who thinks about YRE will see its drawbacks immediately!

2. First of all, quantity is not the same as quality. YRE increases the number of days a student is in school. In and of itself, that means nothing. Half our textbooks are over 10 years old. Teacher turnover is almost 30 percent a year. Student attendance rates are at all-time lows. Dropout rates are at all-time highs. Our schools are facing serious problems! How will forcing kids to spend more days in school solve them? In my opinion, YRE will make our problems worse.

3. Rather than jump onto a questionable bandwagon, we should go back to basics. We should focus on tried-and-true methods of education. We must honor our teachers and celebrate their dedication. We must challenge our students to perform at higher levels. Local and national leaders must make education their number-one concern. Only then will education become a wellspring of pride, not a backwater of neglect.

4. Should year-round education be adopted here, it will cause havoc for families. Under YRE, different children in the same family will have different vacations, or intercessions. Making arrangements for child care will be a nightmare. Mom, Dad, and all the kids will be on different schedules. The whole family won't be able to go away together for a summer vacation because there won't be one. Our families—already under stress—will become more fragmented.

5. There are so many other reasons that YRE is impractical. We live in a very warm climate. Right now, none of our schools have air-conditioning because they're usually closed all summer. Is it fair to ask young people to sweat through July and August? No, it isn't. Installing air-conditioners in the schools, however, would cost millions.

6. Studies also show that after a draining school year, teachers and students need that long summer vacation. It's a time to **replenish** the well. It's the season for relaxation, extended travel, and the chance to do something completely different. Without the good old summertime, teachers and students will be unable to cope with the stresses of the school year.

7. Speaking of teachers, do we expect them to go along with YRE without a salary increase? They'll be working more days. Instead of getting all summer off, they'll have to make do with a few intercessions. Other school workers will have to be paid year-round, too. How much will this cost? Nobody knows for sure, but we should find out before we climb aboard the bandwagon!

28. What is the main idea of Martha Hitt's editorial?

 A. Under YRE, students will attend school for 60 days and then get 20 days off.

 B. Year-round education will save the school district a great deal of money.

 C. Schools are important resources that belong to the people.

 D. YRE will greatly benefit both the school and the community.

29. With which statement would Ms. Hitt PROBABLY agree?

 A. Having the whole summer off has served our nation's students well.

 B. YRE will lead to higher scores on statewide tests.

 C. A school's calendar and schedule don't really matter as long as certain skills are taught.

 D. Schools have very little to offer the community.

30. Which statement is a fact?

 A. Since the schools are always open, they can serve the students better.

 B. Those new buildings would cost at least $40 million.

 C. Schools are too important to close down.

 D. YRE is bound to improve student grades and performance.

31. In paragraph 6, Ms. Hitt compares America today with America 100 years ago in order to show that

 A. some things about summertime and kids will never change.

 B. the present school vacation schedule no longer fits our needs.

 C. year-round schooling has a long history in America.

 D. most kids like to find jobs during school vacations.

32. What is the main idea of Sonny Kwon's editorial?

 A. Most teachers are unlikely to favor year-round education.

 B. Year-round education is a bandwagon.

 C. Making education our number-one priority is more important than year-round education.

 D. Due to various drawbacks, year-round education is unworkable.

33. Which statement is a fact?

 A. With YRE, making arrangements for child care will be a nightmare.

 B. Installing air-conditioners in the schools would cost millions.

 C. Local and national leaders must make education their number-one concern.

 D. Our schools are facing serious problems.

34. With which statement would Mr. Kwon PROBABLY agree?

A. School principals and leading teachers should be featured on local TV shows.

B. New and experimental ways of teaching should be tried out in the schools whenever possible.

C. YRE should be tried for one year to see whether it is effective.

D. The number of days a student spends in school should be raised by 10 percent immediately to improve performance.

35. By the term **bandwagon** in the first paragraph of his editorial, Mr. Kwon means

A. a far-reaching proposal.

B. a popular fad or movement.

C. any vehicle for change.

D. a form of entertainment for students.

36. From clues in paragraph 6 of Mr. Kwon's editorial, you can figure out that **replenish** means

A. draw from.

B. reflect on.

C. refill.

D. enter.

37. A study shows that fewer than 10 percent of the students in the Lincoln School district go to summer camp or on family summer vacations. This detail would

A. mainly support Ms. Hitt's main idea.

B. mainly support Mr. Kwon's main idea.

C. support the main idea of both editorials.

D. not support the main idea of either editorial.

38. Which statement BEST describes the content of the editorials?

A. Ms. Hitt uses mainly facts while Mr. Kwon relies mainly on opinions.

B. Mr. Kwon uses mainly facts while Ms. Hitt relies on opinions.

C. Both use mainly facts.

D. Both rely on a mix of facts and opinions.

39. Do you think Ms. Hitt or Mr. Kwon made a stronger argument? State your opinion and summarize two points that he or she made that you thought were most persuasive.

_____

_____

_____

_____

STOP

These pages from a sales brochure from a mountain bike company will test your skills with everyday text. Read the passage and answer the questions. Mark your answer choices on the answer sheet provided. The clock symbol tells how much time you have to finish the test.

Mastering Your Mountain Bike

Getting Through

Part of the fun (and challenge) of mountain biking is tough terrain. Here are some tips for getting through, over, or down the rough spots.

Loose Rocks Avoid turning the bars to steer. Shift your shoulders instead in the direction you want to go.

Snow Keep the bike in a straight line. Head from firm spot to firm spot.

Streams Make sure you can see the bottom. Switch to a lower gear. Shift your weight back and accelerate.

Sandy Hills Don't expect to freewheel downhill on sand. Soft sand creates resistance, so expect to pedal to keep going. Keep the tire pressure low so you don't dig in.

Obstacles The worst thing to do is hit a log or rock head-on with your full weight behind the bike. Release the front brake long enough to pull back on the bars and lift the front wheel onto the obstacle.

Rules of the Road

1. Ride on open trails only. Stay off closed trails and private property.

2. Don't create new trails. The best riders leave no trace that they were there.

3. Always yield. A verbal greeting or a ringing bell alerts others that you are approaching.

4. Slow down for animals. A spooked animal can be dangerous to you or others.

Sizing Up Your Bike

- **Handlebars** Handlebars should be positioned 1 to 2 inches below the saddle. Wide handlebars offer good control at slow speeds. Narrow ones are better for speed.

- **Seat** The seat post should be exposed by 6 to 8 inches. When going down steep hills, lower the seat slightly.

- **Frame** Think small. Choose the smallest bike frame that gives you a good overall fit. Smaller bikes are lighter, easier to maneuver, and safer.

The Right Tire for You

Choosing the right tires will make your ride safer and smoother. Here are four kinds of tires you can choose from.

The Slick A treadless tire for optimal grip on asphalt and concrete, the Slick provides a comfortable ride, minimal **resistance**, and low tire noise.

The Multipurpose A lightweight tire that is very stable in wet weather. Used off-road, it's suitable for hard-packed surfaces but not mud.

The Knobby 1 The traditional, soft-rubber off-road tire. Well-spaced lugs discharge mud fast and easily. Traction is excellent, but the tire has a short life.

The Knobby 2 An oversized racing tire designed for work on rocky terrain. Its large volume of air provides a comfortable ride off-road.

To Fix That Flat . . .

Flat tires should only delay you a few minutes when you carry an extra tube. To change the tube, release the brake on the wheel with the flat tire. If it's the front tire, trip the quick-release and remove the wheel. If it's the rear wheel, move the chain onto the smallest cog and chainrig, turn the bike upside down, and remove the wheel. Lay the wheel down and use the tire irons to remove the **bead** of one side of the tire from the wheel.

After removing the tube completely from the rim, run your fingers inside the tire to find any sharp object that may have punctured the tire. If you find one, remove it from the outside of the tire. Also pull the tire to one side and check that the rim tape covers the spokeheads. Then insert a new tube and pump in a small amount of air. Using your hands, start at the valve and knead the bead of the tire back onto the rim. If the last few inches of tire refuses to go back on the rim, you may have to use gentle pressure with the tire iron.

Once the tire is on, pinch the sidewalls between your fingers and thumbs all the way around the rim to release the tube should it be caught. Inflate the tube lightly. Then deflate it. Run your fingers and thumbs around the tire again, pinching the sidewalls together. Then inflate the tire hard and replace the wheel on the bike.

Trailblazers!

Once you master your new mountain bike, you might try one of these top courses.

Olympic Mountain Bike Course Take the route of the 1996 Olympic cyclists in north-central Georgia. You'll splash through three streams, soar off man-made drop-offs, and maneuver over slick granite. A loop has been added to the original 6.6-mile Olympic trail to make the course almost 10 miles.

Sun Valley Just outside Sawtooth National Forest, these 320 miles of trails in south-central Idaho give you a chance to ride through muddy creeks, over rough log bridges, and up and down steep mountains.

Everglades National Park Over 37 miles of paved and dirt bike trails and roads wind through southern Florida's famous wetland. You're likely to see all kinds of birds, deer, and even alligators.

Bend, Oregon About 325 miles wind through the alpine forests, desert canyons, and lava rock formations of central Oregon.

Kettle Moraine Close to Chicago and Milwaukee, the 23 miles of this popular trail include challenging loops over glacier-created hills and ridges.

Randolph In the shadow of Vermont's Green Mountains, Randolph's 450 miles of bike trails lead through dark forests and green meadows.

40. Before inserting the new tube, you should
    A. pump in a small amount of air.
    B. check that the spokeheads are covered.
    C. knead the bead of the tire back onto the rim.
    D. remove the bead of one side of the tire from the wheel.

41. You should begin to knead the tire onto the rim at
    A. the spokeheads.
    B. the point of the puncture.
    C. the valve.
    D. the last few inches of the rim.

42. Once the tire is back on, you should pinch the sidewalls between your fingers and thumbs
    A. to find any sharp object that has punctured the tube.
    B. to get the last few inches of tire back on the rim.
    C. to release the tube if it is caught.
    D. to make sure the tire bead is in place.

43. The word **bead** in the directions for fixing a flat tire means
    A. a piece of glass or metal with a hole through it used as a decoration.
    B. a prayer.
    C. a small ball-shaped body.
    D. a rim or band that sticks out.

44. Rita knows she will be traveling through sand on a downhill trail. To get through it, she should
    A. keep the bike in a straight line.
    B. shift her weight back and accelerate.
    C. keep the air pressure in her tires low.
    D. shift her shoulders in the direction she wants to go.

45. Pak wants a mountain bike to ride on the dirt roads near his home. If the area is usually quite dry, he should probably buy which type of tires?
    A. Slick
    B. Multipurpose
    C. Knobby 1
    D. Knobby 2

46. Which reason is NOT given for why you should choose a mountain bike with a small frame?

    A. Smaller bikes are faster.

    B. Smaller bikes are lighter.

    C. Smaller bikes are easier to maneuver.

    D. Smaller bikes are safer.

47. The meaning of **resistance** in the description of the Slick tire in the section "The Right Tire for You" means

    A. fighting against; opposition.

    B. the power to withstand something, such as a disease.

    C. the opposing of one force or thing to another.

    D. the power to oppose the flow of an electrical current.

48. Dan plans to use his mountain bike mainly for racing on hard-packed, level surfaces. He will PROBABLY want a bike with

    A. narrow handlebars.

    B. Knobby 2 tires.

    C. a low seat.

    D. a small frame.

49. Which bike trail featured in the brochure has about the same number of miles of trails as Bend, Oregon?

    A. Olympic Mountain

    B. Sun Valley

    C. Randolph

    D. Everglades

50. Which trail would be most convenient for someone living in the Chicago area?

    A. Sun Valley

    B. Bend

    C. Kettle Moraine

    D. Everglades

51. Brianna wants to combine biking with her annual trip to Florida. Which trail should she consider?

    A. Randolph

    B. Olympic Mountain

    C. Sun Valley

    D. Everglades National Park

52. If you were going to bike on the trails at Sun Valley, what type of tires would you put on your bike? State your reasons.

_____

_____

_____

_____

Identifying Main Idea and Supporting Details

Learn/Review

Most authors write in order to share ideas. To make their ideas clear, authors use details to support or tell more about their ideas.

The **main idea** of a paragraph is the most important point the writer makes in that paragraph. The main idea expresses what the paragraph is about. The sentence that states the main idea is called the **topic sentence**. The other sentences in the paragraph usually provide details that support, or tell about, the main idea. They're called **supporting details**. Often, the topic sentence begins a paragraph, but it can appear in the middle or at the end, too.

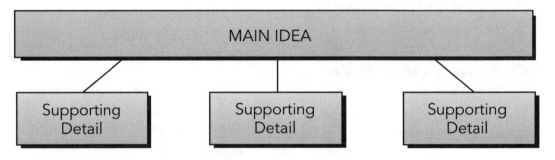

Practice/Apply

Read this paragraph and answer the questions. Circle the letter of the correct answer to each question below.

We're used to ads on TV, radio, and in magazines. Recently, though, ads have begun popping up in unexpected places. In some communities, ATM machines and gas pumps display ads when you withdraw money or pump gas. Some stores now install floor tiles that advertise a product. Grocery stores even place stickers on apples and oranges telling about newly released videos available for rental. Advertisers claim new ad locations help get their messages across.

1. Which sentence states the main idea of the paragraph?

A. We're all used to ads on TV and radio and in magazines.

B. Recently ads have been popping up in unexpected places.

C. Some grocery stores install floor tiles that advertise a product.

D. Advertisers claim new ad locations help get their messages across.

2. Which detail supports the main idea of the paragraph?

A. Most people don't pay much attention to ads.

B. Some restaurants and health clubs now post ads on their walls.

C. Newspapers earn most of their income from advertising.

D. Advertising is a multibillion-dollar industry.

Mini-Lesson 2 Recognizing Cause and Effect

Why is the school football team winning all its games? Why is the President going to China? Why is a new TV show so popular? Writers often write about why things happen. Looking for the reasons things happen will help you understand the events you read about.

Learn/ Review

When one thing causes something else to happen, the process is called **cause and effect**. A **cause** is an event that makes something happen. An **effect** is what happens. As the charts below show, an effect may have several causes. Similarly, a cause may have several effects.

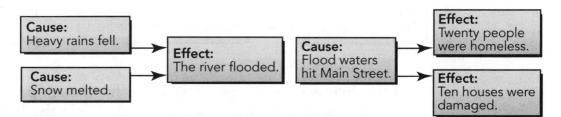

Practice/ Apply

Read the following passage and look for examples of cause and effect. Then answer the questions below. Circle the letter of the correct answer.

The mountain lion once roamed all of North America, and some Native Americans honored it as a god. Early European settlers viewed the big cats differently, however. States offered bounties to hunters who shot mountain lions. As a result, by 1900 the cats had been killed off in the East and hunted to near extinction in the West. Finally, in the 1970s, attitudes began to change when the few remaining mountain lions became a symbol of the vanishing wilderness. To protect them, lawmakers limited the hunting of the big cats. Increases in the size of deer and elk herds, the lions' main prey, also made the lions' protection possible. Today, the mountain lion population in the West is greater than it was 100 years ago. This environmental success story creates a problem, though. About 50 people have been attacked by mountain lions since 1970.

1. According to the paragraph, a cause of the mountain lions' comeback is
   A. the bounties placed on the lions.
   B. being honored as gods by some Native Americans.
   C. increases in deer and elk herds.
   D. more frequent attacks on people since 1970.

2. One effect of the mountain lions' comeback is
   A. greater appreciation for the vanishing wilderness.
   B. fewer efforts by lawmakers to curb the hunting of the big cats.
   C. increased attacks on people.
   D. smaller increases in deer and elk herds.

Making Inferences

Suppose your best friend didn't sit next to you in the cafeteria the way she always does. She didn't look at you when you said hello, either. She didn't even wave good-bye after school. Although she didn't say it in so many words, you'd probably **infer** that she was mad at you.

Learn/ Review

You make inferences when you read, too. Writers don't tell you everything in a text. They expect you to read between the lines and fill in some information for yourself. To make an inference, you combine the clues in a selection with what you already know.

Details from Text	+	Your Own Knowledge	→	Inference

Practice/ Apply

Read the following passages. Use clues from each passage and your own experience to answer the questions. Circle the letter of the correct answer.

Hearing a loud roar, everyone rushed toward the Allens' house. The roof and chimney were smashed in, and a fire had begun to blaze there. Pieces of wood and metal were dropping to the ground. The tip of a wing and a large motor were half-buried in the lawn where a pool of oil was burning. The crowd breathed a sigh of relief as the sirens of fire and police cars sounded in the distance.

1. From the details and what you know from real life, it seems MOST LIKELY that

   A. a meteorite had hit the house.

   B. the Allens' chimney had caught on fire.

   C. an airplane has crashed into the Allens' house.

   D. two cars have collided.

What an exciting game! At half time, the Panthers were leading the Bears, the number-one team, by two touchdowns! At half time, the home town bands paraded proudly. Everyone cheered the team mascot—a high-strung panther that two young men were struggling to control. Suddenly there was a strange hush in the stadium. Players from both teams ran in all directions. No one at all was paying attention to the whistles of the referees!

2. From the details and what you know from real life, it seems MOST LIKELY that

   A. the Panthers have won the game.

   B. a player has been badly hurt.

   C. the mascot has broken loose.

   D. the Bears have scored a touchdown.

Mini-Lesson 4 Recognizing Sequence

If you're like most people, you do things in a certain order every day. For example, you get up, get dressed, and eat breakfast before you leave home. During the day, you probably have a schedule of things to do first, second, and so on.

Learn/ Review

Sequence is the order in which things happen in a story. Being aware of the sequence of events can help you better understand the stories you read. Writers sometimes use time clue words, such as *first, second, next, then, before, after, during,* and *finally* to show sequence. You can use a flow chart like this to list the sequence of events in a story or passage.

Event 1 → Event 2 → Event 3 → Event 4 → Event 5

Practice/ Apply

Read the following passage. Think about the sequence of events. Then circle the letter of the correct answer to each question.

Imagine a nightmare that wakes up the neighborhood. It happened to me just the other night. It all began when I was fighting a blue alligator from Mars. Things got so scary that I began banging on the wall really loud in my sleep. Then Dad woke up downstairs and thought someone was knocking on the front door. Even though it was late, he got up and opened the front door to see who was there. No one was there, of course, but the stars were so beautiful that he stepped out to gaze at them awhile. A few minutes later, while he's standing there lost in the beauty of the stars, the wind blows the front door shut, locking Dad out. Rather than wake up the family by ringing the bell, he decided to crawl in the kitchen window. That wouldn't have been so bad if Mrs. Van Curler next door hadn't been looking out her window at the same time. She was sure Dad was a burglar and called the police! In no time, the flashing lights and sirens filled the street. So, in the end, my dream woke up everyone on the block!

1. While Dad was gazing up at the stars,
   A. the narrator was banging on the wall.
   B. Mrs. Van Curler called the police.
   C. the front door swung shut.
   D. the police arrived with flashing lights.

2. After Dad crawled in the window,
   A. the narrator had a nightmare.
   B. someone knocked on the front door.
   C. he gazed up at the stars.
   D. the police arrived.

Mini-Lesson 5 Comparing and Contrasting

**Learn/
Review**

Which do you like better—pizza or hamburgers? What is the scariest movie you've ever seen? Which of your friends is a better athlete? Without realizing it, you probably compare things all the time in everyday life.

When you notice how things are alike, you are **comparing**. When you notice how things are different, you are **contrasting**. Comparing and contrasting are ways to understand and remember information.

A Venn diagram shows how two things are alike and different. This Venn diagram compares and contrasts a basketball and a soccer ball.

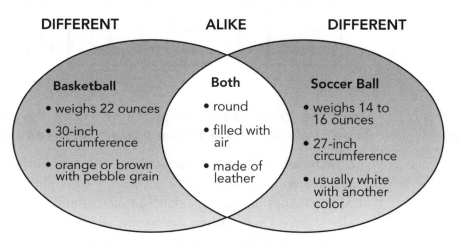

DIFFERENT   ALIKE   DIFFERENT

Basketball
- weighs 22 ounces
- 30-inch circumference
- orange or brown with pebble grain

Both
- round
- filled with air
- made of leather

Soccer Ball
- weighs 14 to 16 ounces
- 27-inch circumference
- usually white with another color

**Practice/
Apply**

As you read this passage, think about how the two types of dragons are alike and different. Then circle the letter of the correct answer.

The dragon appears in the myths and legends of Europe and Asia. Both cultures describe dragons as large, lizardlike animals that breathe fire and have long, scaly tails. In Europe, dragons were ferocious beasts that terrorized human communities. They represented the evils that people fought. In Asia, by contrast, dragons were magical animals and usually good luck, a cross between a lion and an angel. The European dragon lived in dark mountainous caves. In Asia, dragons are associated with the clouds, rivers, and much-needed rainfall. In later times, the European dragon became a ridiculous figure, something to poke fun at. That has not happened in Asia.

1. Both European and Asian dragons
   A. terrorized human communities.
   B. were associated with rivers.
   C. have become ridiculous figures.
   D. were thought to breathe fire.

2. Unlike the European dragon, the Asian dragon
   A. is seen as a lizardlike creature.
   B. represents the evils people fight.
   C. is seen as good luck.
   D. appeared in myths and legends.

Classifying

Why do all the players of brass instruments sit together in the orchestra? Why are tomatoes and lettuce in one aisle of the supermarket, milk and cheese in another aisle, and canned tomatoes and corn in a third aisle?

Learn/ Review

Classifying is grouping items together that have something in common. It's a way to select and organize details conveniently and logically. Often you form **categories**, or groups, when you classify. For example, suppose you wanted to classify the foods you ate today. You might classify the bagel and cereal in the category "Grain Products" and the yogurt and cheese in the category "Dairy Products."

Category 1	Category 2

Practice/ Apply

As you read this passage, think about how the details appeal to your five senses. Then circle the letter of the correct answer.

From a distance, the blue and orange circus tent looked like a giant umbrella floating in the sun. As we drew nearer, a band began blaring brassily, and the crowd roared its approval. Closer still, at the gate, flags were snapping sharply in the breeze. We didn't let the powerfully sweet aroma of cotton candy and candied apples delay us. There'd be time for that later, and we were already late. We gave our money to a giant of a woman covered with pink sequins, and we waited impatiently as she slowly counted out our change. Inside the flap of the tent, the unmistakable scent of elephants and big cats greeted us warmly. "Ladies and gentlemen, children of all ages!" a ringmaster somewhere was bellowing hoarsely. We had no time to look at him, for we were stumbling over feet in the half-darkness, making our way up onto the rough wooden benches.

1. The description of the ringmaster appeals mainly to the sense of
   A. sight.
   B. hearing.
   C. smell.
   D. touch.

2. Which detail appeals mainly to your sense of sight?
   A. the flags
   B. the elephants and big cats

   C. the woman who takes the money
   D. the band

3. Which detail appeals to the sense of touch?
   A. the circus tent
   B. the bench seats
   C. the cotton candy
   D. the flags

Distinguishing Fact and Opinion

What's the difference between these two statements?

- There are 50 states in the United States.
- Texas is the best state in the United States.

The first statement can be proven. You could check a map or atlas and count the states. The second statement shows someone's belief or feeling. You might agree or disagree with the statement, but there is no way to prove that it is true.

Learn/ Review

A **fact** is a statement known to be true or something that can be checked or proven. It is a fact that there are 50 states in the United States. An **opinion** is a statement that expresses a personal judgment, feeling, or belief. Opinions cannot be checked and proven to be true. Often opinions contain judgment words like *believe, best, better, worse, should,* and *probably.*

The ability to distinguish between fact and opinion can make you a better judge of the information that you read, hear, or use.

Practice/ Apply

Read the following passage. Think about which statements are facts and which are opinions. Then circle the letter of the correct answer.

Roundtree Hall was the setting last night for a concert by Violet Express. The band played to a sold-out crowd of over 4,000. The concert was the best live music this city has seen in years! The band's third CD, *No Endings*, has sold a million copies. Jim Maxx, the lead guitarist, was unbelievable. No one else can play with Maxx's power and emotion. The concert began at 9:00 P.M. and lasted almost four hours. After an hour, you could feel the tension and excitement in the hall. The band ended the concert with "Yes, No, Maybe," a tune by Toni Stone. Its smooth harmony and powerful beat brought down the house.

1. Which statement is a fact?
   A. The concert was the best live music this city has seen in years.
   B. The band's third CD, *No Endings*, has sold a million copies.
   C. No one else can play with Maxx's power and emotion.
   D. Its smooth harmony and powerful beat brought down the house.

2. Which statement is an opinion?
   A. Roundtree Hall was the setting last night for a concert by Violet Express.
   B. The band played to a sold-out crowd of over 4,000.
   C. After an hour, you could feel the tension and excitement in the hall.
   D. The band ended the concert with "Yes, No, Maybe," a tune by Toni Stone.

Making Generalizations

Suppose two of your friends who study hard always get A's on tests. Two other friends, who never study, usually get D's. Based on this, you might say, "Studying hard usually leads to good grades on tests." Although you might not realize it, you would have made a generalization.

Learn/ Review

A **generalization** is a rule or statement that applies to many different situations or events. To make a generalization, you take information that you read about in a text and apply the information in a broader sense— to other circumstances or situations. Some examples of generalizations are *Winters tend to be quite cold in the Upper Midwest* and *Few pets require less care than cats.* Generalizations often contain signal words such as *in general, usually, few, some, tend to,* or *most.*

Practice/ Apply

Read the following passage. Then circle the letter of the correct answer to each question below.

Many schools are trying to decide whether to introduce interactive television (ITV) into their classrooms. ITV allows a teacher in one part of the country to teach classrooms of students in other locations using closed-circuit TV lines. ITV supporters say it lets students take courses that would be unavailable otherwise. It also lets great teachers reach more and more students. Opponents claim that the system is too expensive and that the money should be spent on traditional teaching. Another problem is deciding which students benefit most from ITV. What's more, when technical problems arise, students are literally left in the dark. What should be done about that? There's also a more basic question to answer. The personal involvement of a teacher has long been a cornerstone of education. Will students learn just as well from a face on the TV screen?

1. Which generalization might you make from the paragraph?
   A. Much of a school's budget is spent on ITV programming.
   B. Few schools are cutting back their funding of ITV.
   C. Educators must consider many factors before making a decision.
   D. Students prefer ITV to regular classroom teaching.

2. Generalizing from this paragraph, you might also say that
   A. ITV usually adds variety to a student's education.
   B. the personal involvement of a teacher is always better than a face on TV.
   C. for the most part, ITV systems are technically unreliable.
   D. many schools won't use ITV because it will be too commercial.

You won't always have a dictionary at your side when you come across a new word. That's why it's important to use clues in the reading passage to figure out the meanings of unfamiliar words.

Learn/ Review

The **context** is the sentence or passage in which a word appears. Any details in the context that provide hints to the meaning of a word are **context clues**. Here are some common types of context clues:

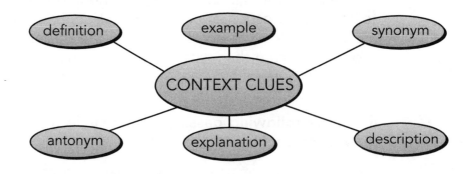

- Sometimes the context clues in a sentence are a **definition** of a new or unfamiliar word.

  > One witness was convicted of *perjury*; that is, <u>he lied under oath</u>.

- A writer might also provide a clue to a word's meaning by giving you an **example**.

  > The patient suffered from *paranoia*; for example, <u>she feared the nurses would strangle her</u>.

- Often, the context includes a word that is a **synonym** for an unfamiliar word.

  > Like George Washington, known for his <u>flawless</u> honesty, our new governor has an *unsullied* record for doing the right thing.

- An **antonym** can also serve as a context clue to a word's meaning.

  > Unlike their *irascible* son, Mr. and Mrs. Mendez are <u>good-humored</u>.

- An **explanation** will often clear up the meaning of the word.

  > One witness in the case may have *perjured* himself: <u>He claimed under oath that he had never met the accused murderer; later, it was learned they were good friends.</u>

- **Descriptions** also contain details that serve as context clues.

  > Except for her bright yellow head, the *cockatiel* had <u>drab gray feathers</u>, but she livened up the room by <u>imitating the speech of anyone who spoke to her</u>.

Read each passage. Circle the letter of the correct answer.

Since huge profits could be made from **pelts**, or skins of fur-bearing animals, Samuel de Champlain realized that a key to French success in the New World was a profitable fur trade. As the fur trade became ever more **lucrative**, it did indeed lead to further exploration and settlement in New France. While this brisk trade improved relationships between French traders and Native American trappers, it tended to **exacerbate** problems between the trading companies and French settlers. By **cultivating** the land—clearing forests and tilling the soil—the settlers drove off fur-bearing animals. Needless to say, this angered the trading companies.

1. Which type of context clue gives you the meaning of **pelts**?

   A. example

   B. definition

   C. antonym

   D. description

2. What is the meaning of **lucrative**?

   A. widespread

   B. popular

   C. profitable

   D. dangerous

3. What does **exacerbate** mean?

   A. solve

   B. worsen

   C. minimize

   D. popularize

4. In this passage, **cultivating** means

   A. improving by care or study.

   B. making friends with.

   C. preparing soil for raising crops.

   D. encouraging or furthering something.

By 1619, settlers in Virginia had begun to demand a greater voice in their government. The London Company sent a new governor to convene a general assembly, and the colonists were instructed to elect burgesses to this assembly. A **burgess** was a person elected to represent a town. Among its first decrees, the Virginia Assembly gave settlers the right to own more farmland. Although Virginia was growing stronger, the London Company was dissatisfied with the profits it realized from the colony. In addition, King James I was not pleased with the colony's management. So, in 1624, the king made Virginia a royal colony, owned and governed by the king or queen.

5. What is the meaning of **burgesses**?

   A. royal colonies

   B. a town's elected representatives

   C. members of a general assembly

   D. colonial governors

6. Which type of context clue helps you figure out the meaning of **decrees**?

   A. example

   B. definition

   C. antonym

   D. description

7. In this passage, **realized** means

   A. accomplished.

   B. got by investment or sale.

   C. made to appear real.

   D. was fully aware of.

GLOSSARY

antonyms: words with opposite meanings

categories: groups of items that have something in common

cause: an event that makes something happen

central purpose: what the author wants to accomplish most by writing the text

characters: the people in a story or novel

character traits: qualities of a character as revealed by his or her words, thoughts, and actions as the story unfolds

classify: to group items together that have something in common

compare: to look for the ways in which two or more things are similar

context: the sentence or passage in which a word appears

context clues: details in the context that provide hints to a word's meaning

contrast: to look for ways in which two or more things differ

effect: the result of a cause

everyday text: the type of writing you see in everyday situations, such as recipes, schedules, and directions

fact: a statement known to be true or one that can be checked or proven

generalization: a rule or statement that applies to many different situations

index: an alphabetical list of items or subjects in a book and the pages on which they are mentioned

infer: to combine details from the text with one's own personal knowledge to reach a logical conclusion

informational text: writing that mainly gives information about a topic

main idea: the most important idea in a paragraph or passage of text

major idea: the important point made in a section of informational text

narrative text: writing that tells a story

opinion: a statement expressing a personal belief, feeling, or judgment; one that cannot be checked or proven

persuasive text: writing that tries to persuade you to do or to think something

plot: the sequence of events that happens in a story or novel

problem: a difficulty or conflict that a character faces in a story

sequence: the order in which things happen in a story

setting: the time and place in which the action of a story takes place

solution: how a character resolves a problem

supporting details: details that develop and explain a major or main idea

synonyms: words with the same or similar meanings

synthesize: to combine the information from one or more texts

table of contents: a list of chapters or other parts of a book and the pages on which they begin

theme: the main idea or message of a narrative text that the author wants the reader to get or think about

topic sentence: the sentence in a paragraph that states the main idea

visual aids: graphs, maps, and tables that organize a great deal of information in an easy-to-use form